English
Olympiad

Class 04

A must have book for all
Olympiads & Talent Search Exams...

by
Dolly Jain

BLoOM CAP
Bloom Cap Edu Ventures Pvt. Ltd.

Bloom Cap Edu Ventures Pvt. Ltd.

卐 **Administrative & Production Office**

'Ramchhaya' 4577/15, Agarwal Road, Darya Ganj, New Delhi -110002
Tele: 011- 47630600, 43518550

卐 **ISBN :** 978-93-25519-23-7

卐 **PRICE :** ₹100.00

卐 **PO No :** TXT-XX-XXXXXXX-X-XX

For further information about the books log on to
www.bloomcap.org

Follow us on   

Preface

"Future belongs to those Who prepares for it today"

School Olympiads are National & International level competitions conducted by different Government, Non-Government & Educational Organisations with the purpose of making the children ready to face competitive exams.

The challenging Questions asked in Olympiads motivate them to learn more & more and bring out the best results with improved academic performance. The Awards & Scholarship offered by Olympiads motivate children to aspire & strive for doing better and emerge out to be the best.

English Olympiads

English is one of the most widely spoken languages across the world. In today's era, good command over English is considered as a must have skill. The greatest advantage of studying English is improvement in communication skills along with the growth of personality.

English Olympiads are meant to strengthen students' command over this universal language by improving spellings, grammar, sentence structure and to master student's language skills.

'Bloom English Olympiad Study Book Class 4' is a perfect resource to Study & Practice for Olympiad Exams and other National & State Level Talent Search Exams & Other Competitions.

Some Special Features of Bloom English Olympiad Study Books are;

- Complete coverage of all the aspects of English; Grammar, Reading Comprehension, Writing Skills, Spellings, Vocabulary & Communication Skills.
- Chapterwise Exercises having different types of Objective Questions at par with the Olympiad Level.
- Olympiad Pattern Practice Sets at the end.

This book is prepared by Expert Panel with the utmost care, still if you have any suggestions regarding its improvement then feel free to contact us at olympiads@bloomcap.org. We will try to inculcate your suggestions in the further editions.

Contents

Noun

Directions (Q. Nos. 1-5) Choose the appropriate collective noun from the options to complete the sentences.

1. A .... of players gathered in the playground.
   - (a) committee
   - (b) team
   - (c) jury
   - (d) bunch

2. My aunt gave me a .... of crayons.
   - (a) box
   - (b) gaggle
   - (c) pad
   - (d) crowd

3. Our .... consists of twenty pupils.
   - (a) chair
   - (b) hall
   - (c) class
   - (d) room

4. Could you pass me the .... of toothpaste please?
   - (a) tub
   - (b) tube
   - (c) pouch
   - (d) bunch

5. We saw a .... of ships in the harbour.
   - (a) herd
   - (b) team
   - (c) fleet
   - (d) army

Directions (Q.Nos. 6-10) Select the kind of underlined noun.

6. <u>Stephen Hawking</u> was born in 1942 in Oxford, England.
   - (a) Common noun
   - (b) Proper noun
   - (c) Material noun
   - (d) Collective noun

7. Abdul Kalam is known for his <u>knowledge</u>.
   - (a) Abstract noun
   - (b) Proper noun
   - (c) Material noun
   - (d) Collective noun

8. <u>Dr. Rajendra Prasad</u> was the first President of India.
   - (a) Proper noun
   - (b) Abstract noun
   - (c) Material noun
   - (d) Collective noun

9. Eating too much <u>sugar</u> can be the cause of diabetes.
   - (a) Common noun
   - (b) Proper noun
   - (c) Uncountable noun
   - (d) Collective noun

10. A <u>gang</u> of robbers looted the bank last night.
    - (a) Common noun
    - (b) Proper noun
    - (c) Material noun
    - (d) Collective noun

Directions (Q. Nos. 11-15) Identify nouns in the following sentences.

11. Saurav bought a new bicycle on Monday.
    - (a) Saurav
    - (b) bicycle
    - (c) Monday
    - (d) All of the above

12. I am going to market to buy chocolates.

    (a) going   (b) market

    (c) I   (d) buy

13. Please give me some milk.

    (a) Please   (b) give

    (c) milk   (d) Both (a) and (b)

14. It is a wonderful day.

    (a) wonderful

    (b) day

    (c) Both (a) and (b)

    (d) Neither (a) nor (b)

15. History is an interesting subject.

    (a) History   (b) interesting

    (c) subject   (d) Both (a) and (c)

16. Match the words in List I with words given in List II to form compound nouns.

	List I		List II
A.	Thunder	1.	Storm
B.	Training	2.	Drill
C.	House	3.	Room
D.	Fire	4.	Keeper

Codes

	A	B	C	D		A	B	C	D
(a)	1	3	4	2	(b)	1	4	2	3
(c)	2	1	3	4	(d)	3	4	1	2

17. Match the masculine noun from List I to their feminine noun in List II.

	List I		List II
A.	Lion	1.	Mare
B.	Horse	2.	Lioness
C.	Bull	3.	Peahen
D.	Peacock	4.	Cow

Codes

	A	B	C	D		A	B	C	D
(a)	2	1	4	3	(b)	2	4	1	3
(c)	2	3	4	1	(d)	2	3	1	4

Directions (Q. Nos. 18-20) Select the correct abstract noun from the given options.

18. (a) Beauty   (b) Beautiful

    (c) Beautician   (d) Beautifully

19. (a) Happy   (b) Happily

    (c) Happiness   (d) Happiest

20. (a) Lovable   (b) Love

    (c) Lovely   (d) Lover

Directions (Q. Nos. 21-25) Choose the correct option to form compound nouns.

21. Down

    (a) Man   (b) House

    (c) Stairs   (d) Hadder

22. Egg

    (a) Bucket   (b) Catch

    (c) Plant   (d) Trap

23. Court

    (a) Convict   (b) Lawyer

    (c) Judge   (d) House

24. Grass

    (a) Hopper   (b) House

    (c) Green   (d) Ball

25. Land

    (a) Down   (b) Slide

    (c) Slip   (d) Air

26. Read the statements given below and choose the correct option.

Statement A: The 'Ganges' is a proper noun but 'Headmaster' is a neuter gender.

Statement B: 'Iron' is a material noun but 'jealousy' is an abstract noun.

    (a) Only A is correct

    (b) Only B is correct

    (c) Both A and B are correct

    (d) Neither A nor B is correct

27. Consider the statements and mark correct sentence True (T) and incorrect sentence as False (F).

    Statement A: 'Eagerness' is an abstract noun.

    Statement B: A 'group' of soldiers is a common noun.

    (a) TT   (b) FT   (c) TF   (d) FF

Directions (Q. Nos. 28-32) Complete the passage using suitable nouns from the given options.

Sachin Tendulkar was born on 24th April, 1973 in Bombay, ...**(28)**........ . Given his first cricket bat at the age of 11, Tendulkar was just 16, when he became India's youngest Test ......**(29)**...... . In 2005, he became the first cricketer to score 35 ......**(30)**...... (100 runs in a single inning) in Test matches. In 2007, Tendulkar reached another major milestone, becoming the first player to record 15000 runs in one-day international games. Considered by many to be the greatest cricket player of all time, Tendulkar took home the ......**(31)**...... with his team in 2011 and retired from the ......**(32)**...... 2 years later.

28. (a) India   (b) a city
    (c) Pakistan   (d) Sri Lanka

29. (a) commentator   (b) cricketer
    (c) captain   (d) coach

30. (a) runs   (b) balls
    (c) rupees   (d) centuries

31. (a) Ranji Trophy
    (b) Ashes Cup
    (c) World Cup
    (d) Asia Cup

32. (a) match   (b) stadium
    (c) pitch   (d) sport

Pronoun

Directions (Q. Nos. 1-15) Choose the correct pronouns to complete the sentences given below.

1. Look at ....
   (a) she   (b) hers   (c) him   (d) their

2. .... is my car. Do you like it?
   (a) These   (b) Those
   (c) This   (d) Such

3. Ryan and Anya have come. ....want to play the guitar.
   (a) Who   (b) Whom
   (c) They   (d) Them

4. .... is her house and this is ....
   (a) This, my   (b) That, mine
   (c) These, him   (d) That, their

5. The paper caught fire and I put .... out.
   (a) my   (b) her   (c) it   (d) you

6. With .... do you share your lunch at school?
   (a) who   (b) where
   (c) which   (d) whom

7. .... is the car which my father presented me on my birthday.
   (a) This   (b) Those
   (c) Whose   (d) None of these

8. The class teacher said to the students," .... have to do your work ...."
   (a) I, yourself   (b) You, yourselves
   (c) Them, I   (d) We, your

9. .... is missing in this book.
   (a) That   (b) Something
   (c) Everyone   (d) Ours

10. .... is a good singer?
    (a) Who   (b) What   (c) That   (d) Mine

11. .... like comedy movies.
    (a) Your   (b) He   (c) It   (d) I

12. What do Sam and his sister have in their breakfast?
    .... have oats in their breakfast.
    (a) We   (b) Them
    (c) They   (d) Theirselves

13. Why is Charlie at the platform?
    .... is at the platform to catch the train to his home.
    (a) He   (b) Him
    (c) Himself   (d) It

14. .... machine can change the world.
    (a) Any   (b) That   (c) Those   (d) These

15. .... are migrating birds.
    (a) Few   (b) That
    (c) This   (d) Those

Directions (Q. Nos. 16-20) Choose the sentence as directed.

16. The sentence with a demonstrative pronoun.
    (a) I am going to Delhi.
    (b) We are playing.
    (c) That belongs to the 17th century.
    (d) She will not come.

17. The sentence with a personal pronoun.
    (a) He works for long hours.
    (b) That lady is my aunt.
    (c) Do your work yourself.
    (d) Is this bag yours?

18. The sentence with a reflexive pronoun.
    (a) She fell down on the floor.
    (b) She hurt herself.
    (c) She is in pain.
    (d) She will not go to school.

19. The sentence with a possessive pronoun.
    (a) This property is vacant.
    (b) This property is not mine.
    (c) This property belongs to Rajat.
    (d) None of the above

20. The sentence with an interrogative pronoun.
    (a) Why do you want to go?
    (b) Where do you want to go?
    (c) Whom do you want to go with?
    (d) All of the above

Directions (Q. Nos. 21-25) Choose the pronouns in the given sentences.

21. Their shoes are under the bed.
    (a) Their   (b) under
    (c) are   (d) the

22. He is a good person whom you can trust.
    (a) He   (b) whom
    (c) Both (a) and (b) (d) can

23. All of the seniors are excited for graduation.
    (a) the   (b) are
    (c) excited   (d) All

24. I had forgotten my wallet in the room.
    (a) I   (b) my
    (c) in   (d) Both (a) and (b)

25. He is planning to hide behind the door.
    (a) planning   (b) behind
    (c) He   (d) hide

Directions (Q. Nos. 26-30) Replace the underlined nouns with the correct pronouns.

26. He taught English to <u>Jack, Jones and Pamela</u>.
    (a) Us   (b) Them
    (c) They   (d) Whom

27. I never want to scold <u>Tom</u> for his mistakes as <u>Tom</u> is a little boy.
    (a) He, Him
    (b) Him, He
    (c) Them, He
    (d) It, Her

28. The headmistress likes <u>Shivani</u> a lot.
    (a) She
    (b) Him
    (c) Her
    (d) them

29. <u>Mitali, Suman and Kavita</u> are planning to go to Jaipur.
    (a) We   (b) They
    (c) Them   (d) Us

30. <u>Asian Lion</u> is an endangered species now.
    (a) He   (b) She
    (c) They   (d) It

Directions (Q. Nos. 31-40) Read the passage carefully and fill up the blanks with correct options.

Once upon a time there was a small hill. People often walked on ......(31)...... to go to a holy place. A girl also climbed the hill with ......(32)...... . Her name was Meena. She was twelve years old. ......(33)...... carried a small boy on her back. ......(34)...... was four years old. Once, a man in the group asked Meena, "......(35)...... child, why are ......(36)...... carring a boy on ......(37)...... back. Don't you feel ......(38)...... load?" Meena could not understand ......(39)...... (Her brother was unable to walk). Meena said, "Load? Of course, not! ......(40)...... is my brother."

31. (a) him   (b) her   (c) it   (d) those

32. (a) that   (b) those
   (c) them   (d) their

33. (a) He   (b) She
   (c) This   (d) That

34. (a) His   (b) Her
   (c) He   (d) Him

35. (a) Mine   (b) My
   (c) Her   (d) His

36. (a) they   (b) them
   (c) their   (d) you

37. (a) our   (b) their
   (c) your   (d) his

38. (a) her   (b) his
   (c) mine   (d) ours

39. (a) his   (b) her
   (c) then   (d) him

40. (a) She
   (b) They
   (c) He
   (d) We

03

Verb

Directions (Q.Nos. 1-5) Fill in the blanks with the most suitable helping verb.

1. Rohan and Sohan .... watching television.
   (a) is   (b) was   (c) am   (d) are

2. .... you believe in God?
   (a) Do   (b) Is   (c) Are   (d) Does

3. Anshi .... recognise people easily.
   (a) is   (b) has   (c) can   (d) was

4. Everybody .... completed their work before time.
   (a) is   (b) has
   (c) will   (d) have

5. It .... rain today.
   (a) may   (b) is   (c) was   (d) has

Directions (Q.Nos. 6-10) Choose the action verb in the following options.

6. (a) Teacher   (b) Teachable
   (c) Teach   (d) None of these

7. (a) Beauty   (b) Beautify
   (c) Beautification   (d) Beautician

8. (a) Encircle   (b) Circle
   (c) Circular   (d) None of these

9. (a) Lightning   (b) Light
   (c) Lighter   (d) Enlighten

10. (a) Serve   (b) Service
    (c) Server   (d) Serving

Directions (Q.Nos. 11-18) Find out the verb in the sentences given below.

11. The policeman failed to catch the thief.
    (a) policeman   (b) failed
    (c) catch   (d) thief

12. A father always helps his children to solve problems.
    (a) always   (b) children
    (c) problems   (d) helps

13. Take a bath before your breakfast.
    (a) take   (b) bath
    (c) breakfast   (d) None of these

14. Being a mother, she is more helpful than a father.
    (a) being   (b) is
    (c) helpful   (d) Both (a) and (b)

15. When Mahatma Gandhi began to speak, everyone became quite in the hall.
    (a) began   (b) became
    (c) Both (a) and (b)   (d) None of these

16. Stacy is washing her dirty clothes.
   (a) dirty   (b) her
   (c) washing   (d) clothes

17. I can't go alone to the market.
   (a) alone   (b) can't   (c) market (d) to

18. You must make this basket to win the game.
   (a) must   (b) make
   (c) win   (d) All of these

Directions (Q. Nos. 19-23) Read the passage carefully and answer the following questions.

All spiders ......(19)...... webs. Webs ......(20)...... spiders to do three things. Webs help spiders to ......(21)...... their eggs. Webs help spiders to hide and to ......(22)..... food. Many spiders like to lay their eggs in their webs. Webs help spiders to ......(23)...... their eggs safe.

19. (a) made   (b) prepare
   (c) stitch   (d) spin

20. (a) support   (b) help
   (c) make   (d) None of these

21. (a) kept   (b) held
   (c) hold   (d) move

22. (a) pick   (b) catch (c) slip   (d) cat

23. (a) put   (b) hide   (c) pack   (d) keep

Directions (Q. Nos. 24-27) Choose the sentence with the correct usage of verbs.

24. (a) Please lent me your spoon.
   (b) I will go to England in order to improve my English.
   (c) She didn't wanted to go to the dentist, yet she went anyway.
   (d) I studies for long hours at night, therefore I got very high marks from the final exams.

25. (a) David is written a novel about wildlife heritage.
   (b) He left his bag here and go outside.
   (c) He is begging to save his mother's life in front of the doctor.
   (d) She was smiled in front of the audience.

26. (a) Everyone likes to watch a magic show.
   (b) You were always tried to jump over the wall.
   (c) I is not feeling well to go to the stage.
   (d) Akhil has playing basketball at the college tournament.

27. (a) They themselves admitted to their mistakes.
   (b) I was planned to hide it under the bed.
   (c) She asked me to reviewing it by this evening.
   (d) This is the lady who help me.

Adverb

Directions (Q. Nos. 1-10) Fill in the blank with the most appropriate adverb.

1. The old man is walking ....
   (a) up   (b) down (c) slowly (d) fast

2. I went .... and found no one.
   (a) daily   (b) quite
   (c) quickly   (d) there

3. The rain fell .... against the window pane.
   (a) heavily   (b) awkwardly
   (c) wickedly   (d) smugly

4. I .... visit my friends as they stay far.
   (a) always (b) rarely (c) daily   (d) now

5. Mother had prepared lunch but we had .... eaten pizza.
   (a) already   (b) first
   (c) only   (d) after

6. Come .... so we can start.
   (a) off   (b) daily
   (c) soon   (d) proudly

7. Please wait ....
   (a) slowly (b) today (c) well   (d) outside

8. It is .... cold outside.
   (a) too   (b) very
   (c) mostly   (d) Both (a) and (b)

9. He left Delhi two years ago and I haven't seen him ....
   (a) soon   (b) since
   (c) today   (d) often

10. People who shop .... can save a great deal of money.
    (a) wisely   (b) beautifully
    (c) frequently   (d) softly

Directions (Q. Nos. 11-15) Choose the adverbs from the given sentences.

11. You should try harder.
    (a) You   (b) should
    (c) harder   (d) try

12. He searched for his key everywhere except his pocket.
    (a) everywhere   (b) searched
    (c) except   (d) pocket

13. They won the game easily after halftime.
    (a) easily   (b) won
    (c) halftime   (d) game

14. The team played the matches brilliantly.
    (a) played   (b) matches
    (c) brilliantly   (d) None of these

15. Luckily, he escaped unhurt by the lion.
    (a) unhurt   (b) luckily
    (c) escaped   (d) Both (a) and (b)

Directions (Q. Nos. 16-20) Choose the suitable adverbs for the underlined words.

16. Brijesh was tall <u>as much as</u> to reach the shelf.
    (a) sufficient   (b) less
    (c) enough   (d) much

17. She goes to work <u>two times</u> a day.
    (a) twice
    (b) secondly
    (c) two way
    (d) together

18. I am <u>many times</u> late for my class.
    (a) always   (b) often
    (c) rarely   (d) never

19. She shouted at him <u>in a furious way</u>.
    (a) fast   (b) furiously
    (c) angrily   (d) loudly

20. In <u>normal</u> circumstances, he would say 'no'.
    (a) lately
    (b) usually
    (c) always
    (d) normally

Directions (Q. Nos. 21-25) Choose the sentence which contains an adverb.

21. (a) I shall go now.
    (b) Water freezes at 0°C.
    (c) My uncle sang his son to sleep.
    (d) He is a fast driver.

22. (a) We are travelling.
    (b) We walked quickly.
    (c) I bought a pair of shoes.
    (d) He dressed himself for the interview.

23. (a) We went to Morocco on holiday.
    (b) The team was brilliant.
    (c) She played piano.
    (d) I'm going to carry the eggs carefully.

24. (a) We watched TV last night.
    (b) She forgot her purse.
    (c) The manager accepted the challenge very nicely.
    (d) The movie is interesting.

25. (a) Officials shared some important information.
    (b) I met a homeless person in New York.
    (c) I like to draw pictures.
    (d) The bus is moving westwards.

Directions (Q. Nos. 26-30) Choose the adverb from the given words.

26. (a) Advice   (b) Popular
    (c) Easily   (d) Lucky

27. (a) Harmony   (b) Truthful
    (c) Annual   (d) Hardly

28. (a) Anxious   (b) Rarely
    (c) Careful   (d) Total

29. (a) Anywhere   (b) Clear
    (c) Common   (d) Simple

30. (a) Cautious   (b) Nice
    (c) Today   (d) Usual

Adjective

Directions (Q. Nos. 1-4) Choose the correct adjectives from the given options to complete the sentences.

1. Please give me a cup of .... coffee.
   (a) hot
   (b) cold
   (c) Both (a) and (b)
   (d) sour

2. I don't like that photo. It looks really ....
   (a) closed   (b) open
   (c) boring   (d) ugly

3. We should eat .... food for better life.
   (a) health   (b) healthier
   (c) healthy   (d) healthiest

4. It's a very .... story. It made me cry when I read it.
   (a) clean   (b) bad
   (c) sad   (d) weak

Directions (Q. Nos. 5-9) Find out the adjectives from the options given below.

5. (a) Beauty   (b) Beautiful
   (c) Beautician   (d) Beautify

6. (a) Brave   (b) Bravery
   (c) Braveness   (d) Bravely

7. (a) Wonder   (b) Wonderful
   (c) Wonderfully   (d) Wonderfulness

8. (a) Calmness   (b) Calmly
   (c) Calm   (d) None of these

9. (a) Care   (b) Carelessly
   (c) Carefully   (d) Careful

Directions (Q. Nos. 10-14) Identify the adjectives in the following sentences from the given options.

10. It is a slow and boring movie.
    (a) movie   (b) slow
    (c) boring   (d) Both (b) and (c)

11. Mobile is a very useful device.
    (a) mobile (b) useful (c) device (d) very

12. Independence day is celebrated on 15th August.
    (a) Independence
    (b) day
    (c) celebrated
    (d) None of the above

13. In India, few people are rich.
    (a) few   (b) people
    (c) India   (d) Both (a) and (c)

14. He is a better player than you.
    (a) he   (b) player
    (c) better   (d) you

Directions (Q. Nos. 15-17) Choose the statement which uses the correctly adjective.

15.   I. The tiger is the fastest animal on the Earth.
    II. The tiger is the faster animal on the Earth.
    III. The tiger is a fast animal on the Earth.
  Codes
    (a) Only I   (b) Only II
    (c) Only III   (d) None of these

16.   I. I would like to have a few sugar with my tea.
    II. I would like to have most sugar with my tea.
    III. I would like to have a little sugar with my tea.
  Codes
    (a) Only I   (b) Only II
    (c) Only III   (d) None of these

17.   I. That car is mine.
    II. These car is mine.
    III. Those car is mine.
  Codes
    (a) Only I
    (b) Only II
    (c) Only III
    (d) None of the above

18. Match the adjectives given in List I with nouns given in List II.

	List I		List II
A.	Beautiful	1.	Burger
B.	Many	2.	Saree
C.	Biggest	3.	Mother
D.	My	4.	Children

Codes

	A	B	C	D		A	B	C	D
(a)	1	2	3	4	(b)	2	4	1	3
(c)	1	4	3	2	(d)	4	3	2	1

Directions (Q. Nos. 19-21) Change the degree of adjectives in the following sentences as directed.

19. Change into comparative degree.
The Nobel Prize is one of the greatest honours in the world.
    (a) Few honours in the world are as great as the Nobel Prize.
    (b) The Nobel Prize is greater than most other honours in the world.
    (c) The Nobel Prize is greatest than most other honours in the world.
    (d) Few honours in the world are as greater as the Nobel Prize.

20. Change into superlative degree.
No other island in the world is as green as Australia.
    (a) Australia is greener than all other islands in the world.
    (b) Australia is more greener than all other islands in the world.
    (c) Australia is the greenest island in the world.
    (d) Australia is the most greenest island in the world.

21. Change into positive degree.
Lucknow is more beautiful than most other cities in India.
    (a) Very few cities in India are as beautiful as Lucknow.
    (b) Lucknow is the most beautiful city in India.
    (c) Lucknow is as beautiful as other cities in India.
    (d) No other cities in India is beautiful than Lucknow.

Chapter 06

Articles

Directions (Q. Nos. 1-15) Choose the correct articles from the given options to complete the sentences.

1. There is no .... match tonight.
   (a) a   (b) an
   (c) the   (d) No article

2. Canada and .... United States of America are neighbours.
   (a) a   (b) an
   (c) the   (d) No article

3. Sujoy's father is an Indian and his mother is .... European.
   (a) a   (b) an
   (c) the   (d) No article

4. Today I bought three pairs of socks and .... pair of jeans.
   (a) a   (b) an
   (c) the   (d) No article

5. I want .... apple from that basket.
   (a) a   (b) an
   (c) the   (d) No article

6. Does your father work at .... University of Delhi?
   (a) a
   (b) an
   (c) the
   (d) No article

7. Are you looking for .... sunsilk shampoo?
   (a) a   (b) an
   (c) the   (d) No article

8. I checked .... mailbox again.
   (a) a   (b) an
   (c) the   (d) No article

9. Can I have .... spoon please?
   (a) a   (b) an
   (c) the   (d) No article

10. Miss Sheena speaks .... Arabic.
    (a) a   (b) an
    (c) the   (d) No article

11. .... idea given by Saumya was accepted by her teacher.
    (a) A   (b) An
    (c) The   (d) No article

12. .... apple .... day, keeps the doctor away.
    (a) A, the   (b) An, a
    (c) The, the   (d) No article, a

13. I enjoy .... Test match when .... India is batting.
    (a) a, the
    (b) an, No article
    (c) the, No article
    (d) a, No article

14. Albany is the capital of .... New York State. People usually speak in .... English there.

(a) a, No article   (b) an, No article
(c) the, No article   (d) None of these

15. Tim lives in .... small village in .... countryside.

(a) a, a   (b) a, the
(c) the, the   (d) the, a

Directions (Q. Nos. 16-18) Choose the sentence with correct use of article.

16. (a) Where is book I gave you on Monday?
(b) Where is a book I gave you on Monday?
(c) Where is book I gave you on the Monday?
(d) Where is the book I gave you on Monday?

17. (a) Jill Abramsan works as a editor-in-chief in The New York Times.
(b) Jill Abramsan works as an editor-in-chief in The New York Times.
(c) Jill Abramsan works as the editor-in-chief in The New York Times.
(d) Jill Abramsan works as editor-in-chief in The New York Times.

18. (a) Mr Bean has a beautiful cat.
(b) Mr Bean has the beautiful cat.
(c) Mr Bean has an beautiful cat.
(d) Mr Bean has beautiful cat.

Directions (Q. Nos. 19 and 20) Choose the correct article for the given words with the help of alternatives.

19. .... husband
.... honour
.... university
.... UK ship

(a) a, an, a, the   (b) a, a, an, an
(c) an, a, an, the   (d) an, an, a, a

20. .... useful book
.... unique decision
.... heir
.... forest officer

(a) an, a, an, a   (b) a, a, an, a
(c) an, an, a, a   (d) an, a, a, an

Directions (Q. Nos. 21 and 22) Match List I with List II and select the correct option.

21.

List I	List II
A. A	1. Honest man
B. An	2. Picture
C. The	3. Sugar
D. No article	4. Red Fort

Codes

	A	B	C	D		A	B	C	D
(a)	2	1	4	3	(b)	1	2	3	4
(c)	4	3	1	2	(d)	3	4	2	1

22.

List I	List II
A. The	1. Book
B. No article	2. Sun
C. An	3. Milk
D. A	4. Important note

Codes

	A	B	C	D		A	B	C	D
(a)	2	3	4	1	(b)	3	1	2	4
(c)	4	2	1	3	(d)	1	4	3	2

Directions (Q. Nos. 23 and 24) Read the following sentences and identify the correct use of article on the basis of T(True) or F(False).

23. Sentence A: He can play the flute.
Sentence B: You are a Hitler.

(a) TF
(b) FF
(c) TT
(d) FT

24. Sentence A : He takes sugar with his tea.

Sentence B : The chess is played by intelligent people.

(a) TF   (b) FT
(c) TT   (d) FF

Directions (Q. Nos. 25-28) Fill up the blanks with the correct article by selecting the correct option.

James Watt was ......**(25)**...... great Scottish engineer of the 18th century. He did not actually invent ......**(26)**...... steam engine. Instead, he greatly improved it. The man named Thomas Savery invented ......**(27)**...... first primitive steam engine in 1698. The man named Newcomen started making steam engines to pump water from mines in 1712. However, Watt is famous for inventing ......**(28)**...... improved version in 1769.

25. (a) a
(b) an
(c) the
(d) No article

26. (a) a   (b) an
(c) the   (d) No article

27. (a) a   (b) an
(c) the   (d) No article

28. (a) A   (b) An
(c) The   (d) No article

Directions (Q. Nos. 29 and 30) Choose the statements(s) with incorrect use of article/s.

29. (i) I have a bag.
(ii) I have pair of shoes.
(iii) I have an umbrella.
(iv) I have an uniform.

Codes

(a) Both (i) and (ii)   (b) Both (ii) and (iii)
(c) Both (ii) and (iv) (d) Both (iii) and (iv)

30. (i) Deepak is a good boy.
(ii) Deepak is a smart boy.
(iii) Deepak is a honest boy.
(iv) Deepak is a laborious boy.

Codes

(a) Only (i)   (b) Only (ii)
(c) Only (iii)   (d) None of these

Preposition

Directions (Q. Nos. 1-10) Fill in the blanks with and an appropriate preposition.

1. There is a cat .... the roof.
   (a) on   (b) in   (c) at   (d) to

2. My parents live .... America.
   (a) on   (b) in   (c) at   (d) above

3. We are waiting .... the train.
   (a) to   (b) at   (c) for   (d) into

4. She lives .... her husband.
   (a) in   (b) on
   (c) under   (d) with

5. Sonia is going .... the school.
   (a) in   (b) to   (c) at   (d) with

6. He can complete the work .... Friday, as he has two days.
   (a) for   (b) by   (c) on   (d) to

7. The Sun is just .... our head .... noon.
   (a) below, to   (b) above, on
   (c) above, at   (d) below, in

8. The doctor advised the children to take care .... their teeth.
   (a) of   (b) about   (c) for   (d) from

9. He is hiding .... the tree.
   (a) below   (b) near   (c) behind   (d) above

10. The plane is flying .... the clouds.
    (a) abroad   (b) above
    (c) after   (d) down

Directions (Q. Nos. 11-15) Find the preposition in the following sentences.

11. The young mother sat among her children.
    (a) sat   (b) among
    (c) her   (d) the

12. You don't need to shout at me.
    (a) to   (b) at
    (c) Both (a) and (b)   (d) None of these

13. Where are you coming from?
    (a) Where   (b) are
    (c) from   (d) you

14. Hurry up! Dinner is on the table.
    (a) Dinner   (b) on
    (c) is   (d) the

15. The dog was hiding under the car.
    (a) the   (b) was   (c) under   (d) car

Directions (Q. Nos. 16-20) Select the sentence which has correct prepositions.

16. (a) I get up in the morning against 6 o' clock.
    (b) You can play video games after your studies.

(c) His father is an employee by an IT company.

(d) He is nothing about my support.

17. (a) The teacher is explaining below some health issues.

(b) The dumping ground is away the riverside.

(c) Where did this letter come about?

(d) The dog jumped over the hurdle.

18. (a) The movie starts at three in the afternoon.

(b) I received a book to Alina yesterday.

(c) When will you think behind the job?

(d) These two guys are selected in the National Congress.

19. (a) Please spread the blanket in the bed.

(b) This is a book about a young girl named Anne Frank.

(c) The rat is hiding on the cupboard.

(d) The money was shared between five friends.

20. (a) There's a bird's nest through my window.

(b) They have a discussion between football.

(c) The football club's success is besides questions.

(d) The black desk is lying between the grey and the white desk.

Directions (Q. Nos. 21-26) Choose the correct prepositions to complete the sentences.

21. Where do you live in Delhi?
I live .... Shalimar Garden in Delhi.
(a) at   (b) about (c) on   (d) inside

22. Where are you going?
I am going .... school.
(a) from (b) into (c) for   (d) to

23. When does your class start?
Our class starts .... 8 o'clock.
(a) in   (b) on   (c) at   (d) from

24. How does Rohan go to the school?
Rohan goes to the school .... bus.
(a) on   (b) by   (c) from   (d) in

25. There is a peephole .... the door.
(a) of   (b) up   (c) in   (d) at

26. I am thankful .... you .... your kindness.
(a) to, for   (b) from, for
(c) from, by   (d) to, by

Directions (Q. Nos. 27-30) Carefully look at the picture given below and find answers for the following.

27. The dog is sitting .... the pond.
(a) in   (b) at
(c) by   (d) behind

28. The birds are flying .... the sky.
(a) over   (b) above (c) about   (d) in

29. The younger boy is sitting .... his brother's shoulders.
(a) in   (b) on
(c) above   (d) over

30. The small girl is carrying a bag .... her.
(a) between   (b) for
(c) with   (d) from

Conjunctions

Directions (Q. Nos. 1-10) Fill in the blanks with appropriate conjunctions.

1. We wanted to go for a walk, ... it rained.
   (a) but   (b) and   (c) or   (d) so

2. Pragya is a good student .... she got a prize.
   (a) but   (b) and   (c) or   (d) so

3. Paula threw the plate .... it broke.
   (a) but   (b) and
   (c) because   (d) yet

4. I would love to have coffee .... tea.
   (a) and   (b) so   (c) or   (d) yet

5. Neither you .... I will go to Agra in the holidays.
   (a) or   (b) nor
   (c) and   (d) but

6. I bought a neck tie .... a pair of glasses.
   (a) for   (b) and
   (c) but   (d) or

7. Put on .... your jacket .... your coat.
   (a) whether .... or   (b) both .... and
   (c) either .... or   (d) neither .... nor

8. He fought bravely .... was killed in battle.
   (a) and   (b) so   (c) for   (d) but

9. The teacher teaches many students .... they can be successful.
   (a) or   (b) but   (c) so   (d) and

10. Jack is poor, ... he is contented with his lot.
    (a) however   (b) since
    (c) and   (d) either

Directions (Q. Nos. 11-15) Read the following statements carefully and choose the option with the correct use of conjunction.

11. (a) Amit and Shyam are reading.
    (b) Amit or Shyam are reading.
    (c) Amit but Shyam are reading.
    (d) Amit nor Shyam are reading.

12. (a) The child was crying, so he had lost his toy.
    (b) The child was crying, but he had lost his toy.
    (c) The child was crying because he had lost his toy.
    (d) The child was crying, if he had lost his toy.

13. (a) Little Johny could not play as it was raining.
    (b) As it was raining, little Johny could not play.
    (c) Little Johny could not play so it was raining.
    (d) Both (a) and (b)

14. (a) This is neither the time for playing or the time for studying.
    (b) This is the time for studying not for playing.
    (c) This is neither the time for playing but for studying.
    (d) This is either the time for playing nor for studying.

15. (a) This is an expensive so useful gift.
    (b) This is an expensive that useful gift.
    (c) This is an expensive but useful gift.
    (d) Both (b) and (c)

Directions (Q. Nos. 16-20) Identify the conjunctions in the given sentences.

16. He is good at both Maths and English.
    (a) both
    (b) and
    (c) is, at
    (d) both, and

17. He is intelligent but he is lazy.
    (a) but   (b) is
    (c) he   (d) lazy

18. He was punished because he did not complete homework.
    (a) punished
    (b) did not
    (c) because
    (d) Both (b) and (c)

19. Even though it rained a lot, we enjoyed the holiday.
    (a) Even   (b) a lot
    (c) Even though   (d) enjoyed

20. I waited up for her until 11 o'clock.
    (a) her   (b) for
    (c) up   (d) until

Directions (Q. Nos. 21-25) Choose the correct option that joins the following pairs of sentences.

21. Do you want coffee now? Do you want it later?
    (a) Do you want coffee now and later?
    (b) Do you want coffee now but not later?
    (c) Do you want coffee now or later?
    (d) Do you want coffee now and also later?

22. She pedaled her cycle faster. It was getting dark.
    (a) It was getting dark because she pedaled her cycle faster.
    (b) Since she pedaled her cycle faster, it was getting dark.
    (c) It was getting dark so she pedaled faster.
    (d) It was getting dark so she pedaled her cycle faster.

23. There is no milk. We cannot have tea.
    (a) There is no milk until we cannot have tea.
    (b) There is no milk so we cannot have tea.
    (c) There is no milk if we cannot have tea.
    (d) There is no milk as we cannot have tea.

24. Ram does not like coffee. Ravi does not like coffee.
    (a) Either Ram or Ravi do not like coffee.
    (b) Neither Ram nor Ravi likes coffee.
    (c) Neither Ram or Ravi likes coffee.
    (d) Ram does not like coffee and Ravi does not like coffee.

25. She is my sister. She is a good friend.
    (a) She is not only my sister but also a good friend.
    (b) She is my sister unless she is a good friend.
    (c) She is my sister or she is a good friend.
    (d) She is my sister so she is a good friend.

Directions (Q. Nos. 26-30) Read the passage carefully and answer the questions that follow.

Games are the most important part of the life of every child; they are ......(26)...... important as studies. ....(27)....... now-a-days children are more inclined towards indoor games, which affects their health. Swimming, jogging .....(28) .... playing any outdoor game improves their stamina ......(29)..... helps them to have a healthy body. ......(30)....... we are unable to indulge ourselves or our children in such outdoor games.

26. (a) and   (b) as
     (c) but   (d) or

27. (a) So   (b) Yet
     (c) If   (d) From

28. (a) so   (b) or
     (c) if   (d) as

29. (a) and   (b) if
     (c) yet   (d) but

30. (a) But   (b) Or
     (c) So   (d) If

Directions (Q. Nos. 31 and 32) Read the passage carefully and answer the following questions.

1. The Scouts were breaking camp.
2. John was hunting for his right shoe.
3. His heart quickened as he pulled out a shoe from under a bush.
4. But it was not his shoe.
5. 'Gary!' he yelled, 'Isn't this your shoe?'

31. Find out the conjunction in line 2 of the passage.
     (a) was
     (b) for
     (c) his
     (d) None of the above

32. Choose the conjunction from the given options which is used in line 3 of the passage.
     (a) as   (b) a
     (c) from   (d) under

Chapter 09

Tenses

Directions (Q. Nos. 1-10) Fill the correct form of verb in the given sentences.

1. I .... a movie yesterday.
   (a) watches   (b) will watch
   (c) was watching   (d) None of these

2. The world .... Yoga Day tomorrow.
   (a) celebrate   (b) celebrates
   (c) celebrated   (d) will celebrate

3. He .... the book.
   (a) read   (b) reads
   (c) will read   (d) All of these

4. The Earth .... around the Sun.
   (a) move   (b) moves
   (c) moved   (d) will move

5. They .... when they are ready.
   (a) came   (b) comes
   (c) come   (d) will come

6. The train .... in an hour, so we hurried up.
   (a) leaves   (b) leave
   (c) left   (d) was leaving

7. Meena .... an accident last month.
   (a) has   (b) have
   (c) had   (d) will have

8. Madhu .... her leg while dancing.
   (a) broke   (b) breaking
   (c) will break   (d) broken

9. Sandeep .... the boxing match against Vijay tomorrow.
   (a) has won   (b) winning
   (c) will win   (d) won

10. Sharmila isn't here as she just .... out.
    (a) went   (b) gone
    (c) going   (d) will be going

Directions (Q. Nos 11-15) Choose the correct form of the verb underlined in the sentences given below.

11. The students are <u>worked</u> hard for their examination.
    (a) work   (b) working
    (c) will work   (d) None of these

12. Neha and her mother were <u>gone</u> to the market.
    (a) go   (b) will go
    (c) going   (d) None of these

13. She was <u>studying</u> in class IV.
    (a) study
    (b) studies
    (c) studied
    (d) None of the above

14. Nisha was <u>gone</u> from school to home in a bus.
    (a) went
    (b) goes
    (c) going
    (d) None of the above

15. When mother <u>walk</u> into the room, Akshay was sleeping.
    (a) walked
    (b) walking
    (c) walks
    (d) All of the above

Directions (Q. Nos. 16-18) Identify the correct tense of the given sentences.

16. Please be quiet.
    (a) Simple Present Tense
    (b) Simple Past Tense
    (c) Simple Future Tense
    (d) None of the above

17. She was waiting for me.
    (a) Simple Present Tense
    (b) Past Continuous Tense
    (c) Simple Future Tense
    (d) None of the above

18. He will be learning his lesson.
    (a) Simple Future Tense
    (b) Future Continuous Tense
    (c) Future Perfect Tense
    (d) None of the above

Directions (Q. Nos. 19 and 20) In the following questions, select the sentence with correct use of tense.

19. (a) The Earth rotates on its axis.
    (b) The Earth rotated on its axis.
    (c) The Earth will rotate on its axis.
    (d) The Earth rotate on its axis.

20. (a) Last Friday, Mohan goes for fishing.
    (b) Last Friday, Mohan went for fishing.
    (c) Last Friday, Mohan will go for fishing.
    (d) Last Friday, Mohan go for fishing.

Directions (Q. Nos. 21-25) Fill in the blanks with suitable tenses as directed in the brackets.

21. This time tomorrow, I .... on the beach. (Future Continuous)
    (a) am lying
    (b) will be lying
    (c) will have been lying
    (d) will have laid

22. When you called, I .... in the garage. (Past Continuous)
    (a) was working
    (b) am working
    (c) worked
    (d) have been working

23. They .... to open a new shop here shortly. (Present Continuous)
    (a) went   (b) go
    (c) are going   (d) will open

24. I .... German last year. (Past Continuous)
    (a) was not learning
    (b) did not learn
    (c) will not learn
    (d) haven't learned

25. By the time we came, she .... the project. (Past Perfect)
    (a) was finishing
    (b) had finished
    (c) has finished
    (d) will have finished

Contractions

Directions (Q. Nos. 1-10) Fill in the given blank with an appropriate contraction.

1. .... like to work for you if you desire so.
   (a) I'd   (b) I'll   (c) I'm   (d) I've

2. .... reading Ngugi O'Thiongo's novel.
   (a) She'll   (b) She'd
   (c) She've   (d) She's

3. You........... do that.
   (a) shouldn't   (b) can't
   (c) aren't   (d) Both (a) and (b)

4. Hari .... granted permission to go out.
   (a) couldn't   (b) aren't
   (c) wasn't   (d) doesn't

5. Sangeeta .... think of ignoring the duties that were assigned to her by her boss.
   (a) weren't   (b) don't
   (c) couldn't   (d) aren't

6. If it hurts you so much I promise, I .... do it again.
   (a) isn't   (b) won't (c) can't   (d) don't

7. One .... intrude in other's privacy.
   (a) mustn't   (b) won't
   (c) cannot   (d) weren't

8. Julian and Charles put on their coats because .... going outside today.
   (a) their   (b) they're
   (c) they've   (d) they must

9. I will not be at school today because .... got the flu.
   (a) I've   (b) won't
   (c) I'll   (d) I'm

10. .... almost eleven o'clock.
    (a) It'is   (b) It's
    (c) Iti's   (d) Its

Directions (Q. Nos. 11-15) Read the following sentences and replace the underlined words using contractions.

11. I <u>will not</u> be ready to go for another ten minutes.
    (a) won't   (b) willn't
    (c) w'nt   (d) will't

12. <u>I will</u> tell you a story about Bob.
    (a) I'ill   (b) Ill   (c) I'will   (d) I'll

13. You <u>shall not</u> speak unless you are spoken to.
    (a) shouldn't   (b) shalln't
    (c) shan't   (d) shallnt

14. <u>I am</u> so hungry I could eat a horse!
    (a) Iam   (b) I'm   (c) I'am   (d) Ia'm

15. <u>Do not</u> put your hands out of the window.

(a) Don'ot   (b) Dono't

(c) Don't   (d) D'not

Directions (Q. Nos. 16-20) Read the following sentences and replace the underlined contractions.

16. <u>I'd</u> like some extra ketchup with my meal.

(a) I had   (b) I would

(c) I could   (d) I made

17. <u>She's</u> such a nice person.

(a) She was   (b) She is

(c) She is not   (d) Both (a) and (b)

18. <u>They've</u> devised a way to deal with him.

(a) They have

(b) They are

(c) They will

(d) They have not

19. We <u>shouldn't</u> judge a book by its cover.

(a) shall not   (b) should not

(c) should   (d) shall

20. We <u>can't</u> wait that long!

(a) can

(b) cannot

(c) could not

(d) None of these

Directions (Q. Nos. 21-25) Choose the option that shows the correct contraction.

21. Does not

(a) Does'nt   (b) Does'ot

(c) Don't   (d) Doesn't

22. Were not

(a) Wer'ot   (b) W'not

(c) Weren't   (d) Werenot'

23. We have

(a) We've   (b) We'ave

(c) Wea've   (d) None of these

24. She will

(a) Sh'ill   (b) She'll

(c) She'ill   (d) Shew'll

25. Had not

(a) Had'nt   (b) Han't

(c) Hadn't   (d) Haddint

Punctuations

Directions (Q. Nos. 1-10) Choose the option with the correctly punctuated sentence.

1. tell me the truth son
   (a) tell me the truth ?
   (b) tell me the truth, son.
   (c) Tell me the truth, son.
   (d) Tell me, the truth, son.

2. oh a sweet chick is playing with a hen
   (a) Oh, a sweet chick is playing with a hen!
   (b) Oh! A sweet chick is playing with a hen!
   (c) Oh, a sweet chick is playing with a hen.
   (d) Oh! A sweet chick is playing with a hen.

3. the students studied these punctuation rule later they took the final test
   (a) The students studied these punctuation rules: later they took the final test.
   (b) The students studied these punctuation rules; later they took the final test.
   (c) The students studied these punctuation rule later they took the final test.
   (d) None of the above

4. anita said to rajesh I have to go out on Sunday
   (a) Anita said to Rajesh, "I have to go out on Sunday."
   (b) Anita said to rajesh, "i have to go out on Sunday"
   (c) Anita said to rajesh "I have to go out on Sunday."
   (d) Anita said to Rajesh, I have to go out on Sunday.

5. ted and Janice who had been friends for years went on a vacation together
   (a) Ted and Janice, who had been friends for years, went on a vacation together.
   (b) Ted and Janice, who had been friends for years, went on a vacation together;
   (c) Ted, and Janice who had been friends for years, went on a vacation together.
   (d) Ted and Janice who had been friends for years went on a vacation together.

6. i met a beautiful european woman
   (a) I met a beautiful , European woman.
   (b) I met a beautiful European woman.
   (c) I met a beautiful European, woman.
   (d) I met a beautiful , European, woman.

7. my grandmother lives across the street from the school

(a) My grandmother lives across the street. From the school.

(b) My grandmother lives. Across the street from the school.

(c) My grandmother lives across the street from the school.

(d) None of the above

8. hey watch out for that car

(a) Hey, watch out for that car?

(b) Hey, watch out for that car!.

(c) Hey, watch out for that car!

(d) Hey, watch out for the car.

9. pritika lives in Australia her brother lives in England

(a) Pritika lives in Australia, her brother lives in England.

(b) Pritika lives in Australia: her brother lives in England.

(c) Pritika lives in Australia, Her brother lives in England.

(d) Pritika lives in Australia; her brother lives in England.

10. tom went to the store to buy bread

(a) Tom went to the store to buy bread!

(b) Tom went to the store to buy bread.

(c) Tom went to the store to buy bread?

(d) Tom went to the store to buy bread

Directions (Q. Nos. 11-15) Choose the sentence with the correct punctuation.

11. (a) Is the lion a brave animal.
(b) Anu has no money in Her purse?
(c) No, I will not do this.
(d) Where are we going!

12. (a) How wonderful the weather is.
(b) Add milk cream cocoa powder in the Eggless cake.
(c) Tennis, is adi's favourite sport!
(d) Bhaskar doesn't speak Hindi well.

13. (a) The train stopped at Chennai, Hyderabad, Nagpur, Bhopal, and Agra before it reached New-Delhi.
(b) The train stopped at Chennai Hyderabad, Nagpur, Bhopal, and Agra before it reached New-Delhi.
(c) The train stopped at Chennai, Hyderabad, Nagpur, Bhopal and Agra before it reached New Delhi.
(d) The train stopped at Chennai, and Hyderabad, and Nagpur, and Bhopal, and Agra before it reached New-Delhi.

14. (a) Arvind was born on October, 18 2004!
(b) Arvind was born on, October 18 2004.
(c) Arvind was born on October, 18, 2004?
(d) Arvind was born on October 18, 2004.

15. (a) We had coffee, cheese, and crackers, and grapes.
(b) We had coffee, cheese and crackers, and grapes.
(c) We had coffee, cheese and crackers and grapes.
(d) We had coffee cheese and crackers, and grapes.

Directions (Q. Nos. 16-20) Choose the correct option to complete the given sentences.

16. The .... sunroof is broken.

(a) cars   (b) car's
(c) cars'   (d) cars's

17. I was surprised to see .... bike outside of my house.

(a) Vickys   (b) Vickies
(c) Vickys'   (d) Vicky's

18. The news said that .... going to rain tomorrow.

(a) it   (b) its
(c) it's   (d) isn't

19. Where did you leave .... bike?

(a) you   (b) your

(c) you're   (d) youre

20. We only sell .... in this fruit shop.

(a) apples   (b) apple's

(c) apples'   (d) apples's

Directions (Q. Nos. 21-23) Choose the appropriate punctuation for the given sentences.

21. What a wonderful match it was.

(a) Comma

(b) Full stop

(c) Hyphen

(d) Exclamation mark

22. He covered a ten mile journey with his bicycle.

(a) Apostrophe

(b) Hyphen

(c) Quotation mark

(d) Comma

23. Sudhas friend invited her for birthday.

(a) Semicolon

(b) Exclamation mark

(c) Apostrophe

(d) Dash

Directions (Q. Nos. 24 and 25) Choose the sentence with incorrect punctuation.

24. (a) The train leaves every morning at 8 a.m.

(b) Mary was out of milk : so she went to the store.

(c) I think you'd enjoy the party.

(d) Can you draw me a map of your street?

25. (a) When uncle Samuel comes to town, we all have a good time.

(b) "I am very tired," she said.

(c) The rhine flows between France and Germany.

(d) Here is my email address : abc@gmail.com.

Jumbled Words and Jumbled Sentences

Directions (Q. Nos. 1-15) Given below are jumbled words. Unscramble the words and choose the correct answer from the options given below.

1. LOTIONUS
   - (a) Lotusion
   - (b) Solution
   - (c) Notlsuio
   - (d) Slotionu

2. OMILEB
   - (a) Mileob
   - (b) Limebo
   - (c) Mobile
   - (d) Bilemo

3. TACTNOC
   - (a) Contact
   - (b) Cottanc
   - (c) Nactoct
   - (d) Tanocct

4. BTTOEL
   - (a) Lebott
   - (b) Belott
   - (c) Tobelt
   - (d) Bottle

5. PAREREP
   - (a) Reparep
   - (b) Prepare
   - (c) Parreep
   - (d) Raperap

6. TENSESNEC
   - (a) Sentences
   - (b) Secentens
   - (c) Nestsence
   - (d) Tenesscen

7. TOTOAM
   - (a) Tomota
   - (b) Motota
   - (c) Tomato
   - (d) Tamoto

8. PANINGHEP
   - (a) Happening
   - (b) Hingneppa
   - (c) Panheping
   - (d) Penpahing

9. LENDARAC
   - (a) Clendara
   - (b) Raclende
   - (c) Calendar
   - (d) Dalencar

10. HARSTIMSC
    - (a) Charmitss
    - (b) Maschrits
    - (c) Trischmas
    - (d) Christmas

11. TCRODO
    - (a) Corotd
    - (b) Rodoct
    - (c) Doctor
    - (d) Tocdor

12. NIDGIN
    - (a) Niding
    - (b) Dining
    - (c) Gidinn
    - (d) Nigind

13. TTENOGROF
    - (a) Torfegont
    - (b) Fogtorent
    - (c) Gorfotten
    - (d) Forgotten

14. ANTFASY
    - (a) Fatnsay
    - (b) Fantasy
    - (c) Fatansy
    - (d) Fatasny

15. AISTSS
    - (a) Assist
    - (b) Asists
    - (c) Asisst
    - (d) Assits

Directions (Q. Nos. 16-18) Rearrange the words to form a meaningful sentence and choose the correct option.

16. Mritunjay/casio/every/plays/Sunday/the.
    (a) Mritunjay plays the casio every Sunday.
    (b) The Mritunjay plays casio Sunday every.
    (c) Every Mritunjay plays the casio Sunday.
    (d) The casio plays Mritunjay every Sunday.

17. meat/and/milk/us/a/gives/goat.
    (a) A meat gives us milk and goat.
    (b) A milk gives us meat and goat.
    (c) A goat gives us meat and milk.
    (d) A goat gives meat and milk us.

18. Pragya/green/dress/wears/a.
    (a) Pragya wears a dress green.
    (b) Pragya wears a green dress.
    (c) Green dress wears a Pragya.
    (d) Green Pragya wears a dress.

Directions (Q. Nos. 19 and 20) Arrange the jumbled parts in a proper sequence to form a meaningful sentence.

19. he saw/through/a fox/the wood/walking/was/him/following.
    (a) He saw a fox walking through the wood was him following.
    (b) Walking through the wood, he saw a fox was following him.
    (c) Through walking the wood, a fox was following him he saw.
    (d) A fox was following him, walking through the wood he saw.

20. Many/people/did not/however/Alex/he/movie/enjoyed.
    (a) Many people did not enjoyed the movie Alex however.
    (b) However Alex did not enjoyed the many people movie.
    (c) Alex did not people enjoyed many movie however the.
    (d) Many people enjoyed the movie, however, Alex did not.

Directions (Q. Nos. 21-24) Read the passage carefully and replace the underlined words with the correct words from the given options.

Once a dog was crossing a brook. He had a <u>ebno</u> **(21)** in his mouth. While crossing, the dog saw his own <u>aimge</u> **(22)** in the <u>retwa</u> **(23)**. The dog thought it was another dog with a bone in his mouth. He barked at the <u>haswod,</u> **(24)** "bow wow, bow wow." As he opened his mouth, his own bone fell into the water and the greedy dog learned a lesson.

21. (a) boen   (b) bone
    (c) nobe   (d) nebo

22. (a) image   (b) igame
    (c) gamei   (d) gaime

23. (a) wetar   (b) tawer
    (c) tewar   (d) water

24. (a) dowsha   (b) shodaw
    (c) shadow   (d) dhasow

Synonyms

Directions (Q. Nos. 1-13) Select the correct option which is a synonym of the word underlined in the sentence given below.

1. The teacher is very <u>angry</u> with the students.
   (a) calm   (b) annoyed
   (c) quiet   (d) cool

2. We went to watch a movie but it was too <u>long</u>.
   (a) sticky   (b) lengthy
   (c) big   (d) short

3. Pragya's great-grandpa is very <u>old</u>.
   (a) friendly   (b) big
   (c) elderly   (d) young

4. The doctor asked the patient to be <u>silent</u>.
   (a) noisy   (b) early
   (c) sit   (d) quiet

5. The girl is plucking the <u>beautiful</u> flowers.
   (a) pretty   (b) ugly   (c) good   (d) nice

6. Children are advised to stay away from <u>fire</u>.
   (a) flames   (b) match box
   (c) cylinder   (d) electricity

7. The students are given a <u>difficult</u> topic to speak.
   (a) easy   (b) hard
   (c) boring   (d) interesting

8. Sherpa Tenzing went to the <u>apex</u> of Mt. Everest.
   (a) bottom   (b) middle
   (c) top   (d) base

9. The father is in a <u>happy</u> mood today.
   (a) laughing   (b) sad
   (c) silent   (d) joyful

10. The sounds coming from Mohit's home were <u>strange</u>.
    (a) funny   (b) unusual
    (c) weird   (d) Both (b) and (c)

11. The <u>smell</u> of that flower is very pleasant.
    (a) plant   (b) fragrance
    (c) petal   (d) None of these

12. Her <u>remark</u> is very rude.
    (a) speech   (b) call
    (c) comment   (d) None of these

13. The <u>odour</u> of your shoes is most unpleasant.
    (a) colour   (b) sight
    (c) smell   (d) looks

Directions (Q. Nos. 14-18) Select the correct option which is a synonym of the word given below.

14. Ancient

(a) Modern　　　(b) Unique

(c) Old　　　　　(d) New

15. Misty

(a) Rainy　　　　(b) Chilled

(c) Wet　　　　　(d) Foggy

16. Lazy

(a) Tall　　　　　(b) Sleepy

(c) Idle　　　　　(d) Quick

17. Freedom

(a) Liable　　　　(b) Liberty

(c) War　　　　　(d) Peace

18. Intelligent

(a) Brilliant　　　(b) Honest

(c) Brave　　　　(d) Handsome

19. Match the words in List I with appropriate synonyms from List II.

	List I		List II
A.	Fame	1.	Error
B.	Mistake	2.	Recognise
C.	Identify	3.	Glory
D.	Enforced	4.	Applied

Codes

	A	B	C	D
(a)	3	1	2	4
(b)	1	2	3	4
(c)	4	3	2	1
(d)	3	1	4	2

20. Match the underlined words given in List-I with their synonyms given in List-II.

	List I		List II
A.	Don't <u>stare</u> at anyone on the road.	1.	Honour
B.	We should <u>respect</u> our elders.	2.	Foolish
C.	She has made a <u>silly</u> mistake.	3.	Travel
D.	The <u>journey</u> to Goa was amazing.	4.	Gaze

Codes

	A	B	C	D
(a)	2	1	3	4
(b)	3	4	2	1
(c)	1	4	3	2
(d)	4	1	2	3

Antonyms

Directions (Q. Nos. 1-5) Select the option which is an antonym of the word underlined in the sentence.

1. The King of Persia was very <u>kind</u>.
   (a) brave   (b) rich
   (c) cruel   (d) modest

2. Earthquakes are <u>frequent</u> in Nepal.
   (a) extinct   (b) many
   (c) rare   (d) usual

3. Arjun was the <u>younger</u> brother of Bheem.
   (a) bigger   (b) longer
   (c) smaller   (d) elder

4. There will be a/an <u>oral</u> exam on Monday.
   (a) written   (b) reading
   (c) listening   (d) None of these

5. There is a <u>dead</u> snake in the park.
   (a) alive   (b) lovely
   (c) big   (d) survive

Directions (Q. Nos. 6-13) Select the option which is an antonym of the word given below.

6. Hard
   (a) Rude   (b) Tough
   (c) Soft   (d) None of these

7. Decrease
   (a) Increase   (b) Lessen
   (c) Reduce   (d) Lower

8. Pass
   (a) Success   (b) Victory
   (c) Win   (d) Fail

9. Dirty
   (a) Dark   (b) Clean
   (c) Filthy   (d) Dull

10. Sorrow
    (a) Grief   (b) Sadness
    (c) Happiness   (d) Trouble

11. Employment
    (a) Business   (b) Unemployment
    (c) Service   (d) Occupation

12. Important
    (a) Worthless
    (b) Essential
    (c) Valuable
    (d) Chief

13. Full
    (a) Plentiful
    (b) Saturated
    (c) Loud
    (d) Empty

Directions (Q. Nos. 14-18) Choose the prefix that would be added to the given word to form its antonym.

14. Balance
   (a) Im   (b) In
   (c) Mis   (d) Il

15. Certain
   (a) Il   (b) Un
   (c) Dis   (d) Ir

16. Honest
   (a) Il   (b) Un
   (c) Mis   (d) Dis

17. Fortune
   (a) Im   (b) Il
   (c) Mis   (d) Anti

18. Decent
   (a) Anti
   (b) Aut
   (c) In
   (d) Un

Directions (Q. Nos. 19-21) Find the word that is antonym of the word underlined in the sentence.

19. Rohan is very <u>healthy</u> but his younger brother Sohan is not.
   (a) delicate
   (b) poor
   (c) weak
   (d) None of these

20. Everybody wants to succeed because nobody likes <u>failure</u>.
   (a) happy
   (b) success
   (c) joyous
   (d) None of the above

21. We should not discuss our personal life in <u>public</u>.
   (a) secret   (b) private
   (c) open   (d) None of these

22. Match the words with their correct antonyms.

	List I (Word)		List II (Antonym)
A.	Natural	1.	Easy
B.	Difficult	2.	Artificial
C.	Soft	3.	Prosperity
D.	Adversity	4.	Hard

Codes

	A	B	C	D		A	B	C	D
(a)	2	3	1	4	(b)	2	1	4	3
(c)	3	2	1	4	(d)	2	4	1	3

23. Match the underlined word given in the List-I with their appropriate antonyms given in List-II.

	List I		List II
A.	His way of presentation is <u>unique</u> .	1.	Forego
B.	They tried to <u>hide</u> the ultimate reset.	2.	Optional
C.	The role of the police is to <u>enforce</u> the low.	3.	Common
D.	He did not want the guidelines to be <u>mandatory</u>.	4.	Reveal

Codes

	A	B	C	D		A	B	C	D
(a)	1	2	3	4	(b)	4	3	2	1
(c)	2	1	4	3	(d)	3	4	1	2

One Word Substitution

Directions (Q.Nos. 1-10) Choose the best option to fill in the blanks.

1. The person who sells medicines is ....
   - (a) a mediciner
   - (b) a practitioner
   - (c) a doctor
   - (d) a chemist

2. The person who sells meat is ....
   - (a) a butcher
   - (b) a meatier
   - (c) a grocer
   - (d) a cutter

3. One who does not believe in God is ....
   - (a) a traitor
   - (b) an astronomer
   - (c) an atheist
   - (d) a scientist

4. A tool with which a nail is inserted into a wall is a ....
   - (a) pliers
   - (b) hammer
   - (c) screw driver
   - (d) spade

5. Rohini manages the Oxford Amnesty library. She is a ....
   - (a) librarian
   - (b) peon
   - (c) headmaster
   - (d) teacher

6. King Alexander couldn't be conquered, so he is ....
   - (a) inexplicable
   - (b) invincible
   - (c) indelible
   - (d) incredible

7. A/an .... is one who writes the life story of another person.
   - (a) curator
   - (b) author
   - (c) biographer
   - (d) novelist

8. A .... is kept in memory of an event or place.
   - (a) moment
   - (b) souvenir
   - (c) gift
   - (d) maiden

9. A person to whom something is addressed is called ....
   - (a) speaker
   - (b) addresser
   - (c) guest
   - (d) addressee

10. The art of beautiful handwriting is known as ....
    - (a) calligraphy
    - (b) cosmology
    - (c) waiting
    - (d) autobiography

Directions (Q. Nos. 11-20) Choose the best option for the given phrase.

11. One who is incharge of a museum.
    - (a) Curator
    - (b) Caretaker
    - (c) Supervisor
    - (d) Warden

12. A man who wastes his money on luxury.
    - (a) Notorious
    - (b) Versatile
    - (c) Ornithologist
    - (d) Extravagant.

13. A place for housing cars is called ....
    (a) Hostel   (b) Garage
    (c) Auditorium   (d) Kennel

14. A disease which attacks many people in a particular area in one time.
    (a) Epidemic   (b) Pandemic
    (c) Sardonic   (d) Academic

15. One who is new to a profession.
    (a) Novice   (b) Colleagues
    (c) Worker   (d) Recluse

16. That which cannot be satisfied.
    (a) Desire   (b) Immortal
    (c) Insatiable   (d) Posthumous

17. A place where dead person's body is cremated.
    (a) Cemetery   (b) Dormitory
    (c) Crematorium   (d) Hangar

18. A speech delivered without any previous preparation.
    (a) Extempore   (b) Elocution
    (c) Dialogue   (d) Dialect

19. A woman whose husband is dead.
    (a) Widow   (b) Widower
    (c) Bachelor   (d) Spinster

20. A child who does not have parents.
    (a) Orphan   (b) Alone
    (c) Atheist   (d) Ascetic

Directions (Q. Nos. 21-25) Replace the underlined group of words with a suitable word.

21. His uncle is a famous <u>designer of buildings</u>.
    (a) architect
    (b) engineer
    (c) contractor
    (d) builder

22. If you lose your <u>good name</u>, it is not easy to get it back.
    (a) rapport
    (b) reputation
    (c) confidence
    (d) anxiety

23. My friend had the <u>special advantage</u> of visiting England as the official guest of the Queen.
    (a) advantage   (b) amenity
    (c) quality   (d) privilege

24. The Mona Lisa is the <u>best among the works</u> of Leonardo da Vinci.
    (a) painting   (b) masterpiece
    (c) best   (d) beautiful

25. There was no <u>scarcity of food</u> in our country during the last twenty years.
    (a) famine   (b) shortage
    (c) drought   (d) flood

Chapter 16

Word Pair and Odd One Out

Directions (Q. Nos. 1-5) Choose which of the following is NOT a word pair.

1. (a) This and that   (b) Girl and boy
   (c) Pot and spoons   (d) Day and night

2. (a) Salt and pepper
   (b) Soft and silky
   (c) Trousers and socks
   (d) Bed and breakfast

3. (a) Hot and cold
   (b) Life or death
   (c) Lost and found
   (d) Spring and winter

4. (a) Mother and father
   (b) Bread and pickles
   (c) Uncle and aunt
   (d) Cup and saucer

5. (a) Hot and chilly
   (b) Eyes and ears
   (c) Fruits and vegetables
   (d) Hands and feet

Directions (6-10) Select the most appropriate choice in each questions.

6. Busy : Bee :: Gentle :?
   (a) Cat   (b) Peacock
   (c) Cotton   (d) Dove

7. Shoe : lace :: Curtains :
   (a) Rings   (b) Blinds(c) Cover   (d) Cloth

8. Dirt : Fly :: .... : Butterfly
   (a) Nectar   (b) Flower
   (c) Juice   (d) Wing

9. Rupee : India :: .... : Japan
   (a) Rand   (b) Yen
   (c) Euro   (d) Dollar

10. Doctor : Clinic :: .... : Bank
    (a) Librarian   (b) Teacher
    (c) Surgeon   (d) None of these

Directions (Q. Nos. 11-15) Choose the option which has same relationship as given in the question.

11. Work : Earn
    (a) Influence : Assist
    (b) Expect : Think
    (c) Tender : Lovable
    (d) Plant : Harvest

12. Aeroplane : Flying
    (a) Sailboat : Harbour
    (b) Ship : Sailing
    (c) Glider : Park
    (d) None of the above

13. Heat : Cooked
    (a) Cold : Frozen
    (b) Ice : Skating
    (c) Cold : Ice-cream
    (d) Chilly : Thaw

14. Claw : Cat
    (a) Cat : Whiskers   (b) Wag : Tail
    (c) Tail : Dog   (d) Tooth : Bite

15. Pencil : Write
    (a) Knife : Grind   (b) Spoon : Stir
    (c) Fork : Cut   (d) Pen : Ink

Directions (Q. Nos. 16-20) Find the odd word from the following.

16. (a) Praise   (b) Approve
    (c) Laud   (d) Offer

17. (a) Apt   (b) Tender
    (c) Fit   (d) Right

18. (a) Himalaya   (b) Delhi
    (c) Lucknow   (d) New York

19. (a) Book   (b) Pen
    (c) Table   (d) Pencil

20. (a) Success   (b) Failure
    (c) Win   (d) Victory

Directions (Q. Nos. 21-25) The questions given below contain four options with parts of speech. Find the odd one out.

21. (a) If   (b) Before
    (c) Have   (d) Unless

22. (a) Petrol   (b) Diesel
    (c) Truck   (d) Kerosene

23. (a) Forgive and forget
    (b) Tick-tack
    (c) Sweet and sour
    (d) Dear-deer

24. (a) Since   (b) Often
    (c) From   (d) Upon

25. (a) River   (b) Ganga
    (c) Yamuna   (d) Kaveri

Chapter 17

Spellings

Directions (Q. Nos. 1-15) Select the correctly spelt word from the options given below.

1. (a) Beautyfully (b) Beautifully
   (c) Beautifuly (d) Beautyfuly

2. (a) Habitt (b) Habiit
   (c) Habite (d) Habit

3. (a) Success (b) Sucess
   (c) Succes (d) Succass

4. (a) Adres (b) Adress
   (c) Address (d) Addres

5. (a) College (b) Collige
   (c) Colege (d) Colleg

6. (a) Brakefast (b) Breakfast
   (c) Breakfust (d) Breekfast

7. (a) Carpenter (b) Carpantar
   (c) Caurpentur (d) Carpentar

8. (a) Vaiter (b) Waitur
   (c) Waiter (d) Weiter

9. (a) Railwey (b) Railway
   (c) Ralway (d) Raleway

10. (a) Paaspurt (b) Paasport
    (c) Pasport (d) Passport

11. (a) Illuminate (b) Illuminiate
    (c) Illuminaete (d) Illumenate

12. (a) Apetiser (b) Appiteser
    (c) Appetiser (d) Appitesre

13. (a) Vegilance (b) Vigilance
    (c) Vigelence (d) Vigilence

14. (a) Adjacent (b) Adjecent
    (c) Adjecent (d) Adjacant

15. (a) Justefy (b) Jastifi
    (c) Justify (d) Jastefi

Directions (Q. Nos. 16-25) Choose the options with correct spelling to fill the blanks.

16. He .... her that she would pass.
    (a) insurad (b) ensured
    (c) ensourad (d) iensurad

17. It is a story of two men and a batch of .... cars.
    (a) destroyed (b) distrouyid
    (c) diistroyad (d) deistroyied

18. We will have to find an .... source of energy in the future.
    (a) altarnat (b) alternate
    (c) allterrnete (d) allternate

19. Do you .... in magic?
    (a) bilive (b) beleive
    (c) believe (d) None of these

20. Please give me a .... of paper.
    (a) peece (b) piece
    (c) piese (d) peace

21. He came here today and went out ....
  (a) immediately   (b) imediately
  (c) immidiately   (d) imidiately

22. you look .... pale, are you sick?
  (a) extreemly   (b) extrimly
  (c) extremely   (d) extremly

23. Just go home and bring me my .... bag.
  (a) favrite   (b) favourite
  (c) favourate   (d) faverite

24. It has become much more .... than before.
  (a) dangeras   (b) dangrous
  (c) dangeres   (d) dangerous

25. I .... my hands while cooking.
  (a) barned   (b) burned
  (c) burnd   (d) bunned

Directions (Q. Nos. 26-35) Fill in the blanks with right alphabet to make correctly spelt words.

26. An_e_
  (a) p, t   (b) r, g
  (c) g, r   (d) t, r

27. _ki_ _
  (a) S, l, t   (b) L, s, t
  (c) S, s, l   (d) S, l, l

28. Ow_ _ r
  (a) e, n   (b) n, e
  (c) e, e   (d) n, n

29. T_p_er
  (a) o, p   (b) p, o
  (c) e, p   (d) r, p

30. k_t_
  (a) e, s   (b) e, e
  (c) i, e   (d) Q, i

31. g_a_m_r
  (a) r, m, e   (b) r, e, e
  (c) r, m, a   (d) r, e, a

32. _ yc _ _ ng
  (a) C, l, i   (b) c, l, l
  (c) S, l, y   (d) c, l, y

33. _x_ mpl_
  (a) a, e, e   (b) e, a, e
  (c) a, e, a   (d) e, e, e

34. S_me_h_ng
  (a) o, t, i   (b) e, t, e
  (c) a, t, y   (d) e, t, y

35. Ca_ _r _
  (a) n, n, i   (b) n, n, y
  (c) n, a, y   (d) e, e, y

Chapter 18

Idiom, Phrases and Proverb

Directions (Q. Nos. 1-15) Choose the correct meaning of the idiom/phrase or proverb.

1. Seeing eye to eye
   - (a) Treating someone with respect
   - (b) Paying close attention to something someone is saying
   - (c) Agreeing with somebody
   - (d) Identifying a minor mistake

2. A hard nut to crack
   - (a) A difficult problem
   - (b) An interesting problem
   - (c) A unique problem
   - (d) A simple problem

3. Spill the beans
   - (a) To be untidy
   - (b) To reveal something that is supposed to be kept a secret
   - (c) To be very talkative
   - (d) To leave a place quickly

4. Give him a piece of my mind
   - (a) Pardon him
   - (b) Make him my friend
   - (c) Scold him
   - (d) Take him into confidence

5. A lame excuse
   - (a) Useless talk
   - (b) Ill feeling
   - (c) Good explanation
   - (d) Unsatisfactory explanation

6. Got down to business
   - (a) Joined his father's business
   - (b) Become businesslike
   - (c) Began to work seriously
   - (d) Started a business

7. Throw dust into my eyes
   - (a) Abuse me
   - (b) Cheat me
   - (c) Hurt me
   - (d) Terrify me

8. To feather one's nest
   - (a) To build one's house
   - (b) To harbour ill-feeling
   - (c) To get something in abundance
   - (d) To enrich oneself when opportunity occurs

9. To have an axe to grind
   - (a) To fail to arouse interest
   - (b) To have no result
   - (c) To work for both sides
   - (d) A private end to serve

10. Around the clock
(a) Early morning
(b) At different timings
(c) Day and night
(d) Throughout the afternoon

11. Having your heads in the clouds
(a) Day dreaming or not paying attention
(b) To look at the clouds
(c) To pay attention to the galaxy
(d) To enjoy rainy season

12. Spin a yarn
(a) Do weaving work
(b) Tell a long far-fetched story
(c) Be a sunning craftsman
(d) Stay silent

13. Have a blast
(a) Cause an accident
(b) Enjoy a ride
(c) To enjoy oneself
(d) To blast a bomb

14. To end in smoke
(a) To make completely understand
(b) To be ruined
(c) To excite great applause
(d) To overcome someone

15. To hit the nail right on the head
(a) To do the right thing
(b) To destroy one's reputation
(c) To announce one's fixed views
(d) To teach someone a lesson

Directions (Q. Nos. 16-25) Fill in the blanks with the correct phrase.

16. The plane .... at 8 a.m.
(a) took away   (b) took up
(c) took off   (d) took after

17. .... the tiny bits of paper lying on the floor.
(a) pick out   (b) pick down
(c) pick away   (d) pick up

18. They have .... the electricity connection as the Mehras have not paid the bills.
(a) fall out   (b) turned off
(c) cut off   (d) sorted out

19. Is it wise to .... appearances?
(a) go with   (b) go by
(c) go down   (d) go for

20. Ram .... with his practice in order to excel.
(a) went on   (b) went out
(c) went off   (d) went up

21. Make sure that you .... at least two hours before your flight is due.
(a) check off   (b) check out
(c) check up   (d) check in

22. The teacher .... an explanation of his conduct.
(a) called off   (b) called for
(c) called in   (d) called out

23. The publishers are planning to .... a cheap edition of their new dictionary.
(a) bring up   (b) bring in
(c) bring out   (d) bring about

24. She .... the orphan as her own child.
(a) brought up   (b) brought out
(c) brought in   (d) brought about

25. The question .... before the municipal corporation last week.
(a) came out   (b) came up
(c) came off   (d) came in

Reading Comprehension

Passage 1

Directions (Q. Nos. 1-5) Read the following passage carefully and answer the questions that follow. Choose the correct answer from the options given below.

Dolphins are marine mammals, that are related to whales and porpoises. A marine mammal is one that lives in water. Dolphins are found all over the world's oceans as well as in rivers and marshes. Dolphins are carnivores and feed on fish, squid and other marine life. They often swim together in groups called 'pods'.

They are thought to have powerful eyesight and hearing, but do not have a sense of smell.

Dolphins come in different sizes. Some are smaller than the average person, but others, such as the 'Orca', can be 30 feet long or more than five times as long as the average person. Dolphins are thought to be very intelligent and communicate with each other using clicks and whistles. All dolphins are powerful swimmers. Have you ever seen a dolphin? Groups of dolphins can often be seen bobbing in and out of waves close to the shoreline.

1. Dolphins are a close relative of ....
   - (a) fishes
   - (b) carnivores
   - (c) whales
   - (d) mammals

2. Which statement is NOT true about dolphins, according to the passage?
   - (a) They are related to whales and porpoises.
   - (b) They are very intelligent.
   - (c) They bob in and out of waves.
   - (d) They are not friendly to humans.

3. Dolphins do not ....
   - (a) have good hearing
   - (b) communicate
   - (c) have good eye sight
   - (d) have a sense of smell

4. Find the opposite of 'carnivores' from the options.
   - (a) cannibal
   - (b) herbivores
   - (c) meat eater
   - (d) killer

5. Find the synonym of 'intelligent' from the options.
(a) dull
(b) unintelligent
(c) stupid
(d) brilliant

Passage 2

Directions (Q. Nos. 6-10) Read the following passage carefully and answer the questions that follow. Choose the correct answer from the options given below.

Rainbows are often seen, when the Sun comes out after or during a rainstorm. Rainbows are caused when sunlight shines through drops of water in the sky at a specific angle. When white sunlight enters a raindrop, it exits the raindrop into different colours.

When light exits lots of different raindrops at different angles, it produces the red, orange, yellow, green, blue, indigo and violet colour that you see in a rainbow. Together, these colours are known as the spectrum. These colours can sometimes be seen in waterfalls and fountains as well.

6. Rainbows are often seen ....
(a) after a rainstorm
(b) before a rainstorm
(c) after the sunsets
(d) in the dark

7. The colour which is not seen in a rainbow, is ....
(a) yellow
(b) indigo
(c) orange
(d) pink

8. The colours of a rainbow are known as the ....
(a) light
(b) spectrum
(c) beam
(d) None of the above

9. Choose the word from the options which can replace "often" in the passage.
(a) generally
(b) regularly
(c) usually
(d) All of the above

10. Choose the antonym of 'exits' from the options given below.
(a) enters
(b) radiates
(c) goes
(d) glows

Poem 1

Directions (Q. Nos. 11-15) Read the poem and answer the questions that follow. Choose the correct answer from the options given below.

A snake can glide from side to side.
They're really long and like to hide.
They have long backbones, but no hair.
They use their tongues to taste the air.
They taste your scent if you are near,
And hiss a threat for you to hear.
It's wise of you to clear their way,
So you don't have an awful day!

11. Find the correct statement from the given options.
(a) The snake hisses when it threatens you.
(b) The snake runs away when it is threatened.
(c) The snake bites when it is in danger.
(d) The snake uses its tongue when it is hungry.

12. The poet thinks people should ....
(a) pick up snakes
(b) stay away from snakes
(c) wear boots when you walk by snakes
(d) keep snakes as pets

13. Find the incorrect statement from the following options.

(a) Snakes use their tongue to taste the air.

(b) They glide from side to side.

(c) They have long backbones.

(d) None of the above

14. Find the best meaning for the word "scent" as used in the passage.

(a) smell   (b) body

(c) spray   (d) arm

15. Find the opposite of wise from the following options.

(a) intelligent

(b) nonsense

(c) foolish

(d) smart

Poem 2

Directions (Q. Nos. 16-20) Read the poem and answer the questions that follow. Choose the correct answer from the options given below.

Granny, Granny
Please comb my hair,
You always take your time,
You always take such care,
You put me to sit on a cushion between
Your knees,
You rub a little coconut oil
Parting gentle as a breeze
Mummy, mummy
She's always in a hurry hurry rush

She pulls my hair sometimes she tugs.
But Granny,
You have all the time in the world
And when you're finished
You always turn my head and say,
"Now, who's a nice girl"?

—Grace Nicholas

16. What request is made to the grandmother?

(a) To comb her hair

(b) To fold her clothes

(c) To play with her

(d) To dress the doll

17. What is true according to the poem?

(a) The girl loves her mother a lot.

(b) The girl dislikes it when her grandmother oils her hair.

(c) The girl loves her grandmother.

(d) The girl is allergic to coconut oil.

18. Who is in a "hurry hurry rush"?

(a) Mother   (b) Father

(c) Grand Mother   (d) Grand Father

19. What does mother do in her hurry?

(a) She cooks food.

(b) She pulls her hair.

(c) She dances.

(d) She ties a ribbon.

20. What are the qualities that the girl associates with her grandmother?

(a) Love and care

(b) Attention

(c) Anger and sympathy

(d) None of the above

Chapter
20

Spoken and Written Expression

Directions (Q. Nos. 1-10) Select the correct option that defines the following sentences.

1. Could I help you?
   - (a) Request
   - (b) Command
   - (c) Offering help
   - (d) Invitation

2. Complete the work now.
   - (a) Command
   - (b) Request
   - (c) Invitation
   - (d) Apology

3. Would you like to come to the exhibition?
   - (a) Giving an offer
   - (b) Asking for help
   - (c) Asking for permission
   - (d) Asking for directions

4. I am sorry I can't. I have to study at that time.
   - (a) Apologising
   - (b) Refusing an invitation
   - (c) Refusing to apologise
   - (d) Refusing to work

5. How well she sings!
   - (a) Enquiry
   - (b) Appreciation
   - (c) Order
   - (d) Permission

6. Please be seated.
   - (a) Invitation
   - (b) Order
   - (c) Suggestion
   - (d) Request

7. Don't make a noise.
   - (a) Request
   - (b) Order
   - (c) Offer
   - (d) Suggestion

8. Let us go for a walk.
   - (a) Invitation
   - (b) Request
   - (c) Command
   - (d) Suggestion

9. I am sorry.
   - (a) Apologising
   - (b) Accepting help
   - (c) Accepting command
   - (d) Accepting suggestion

10. Can you bring me a glass of water?
    - (a) Asking for help
    - (b) Request
    - (c) Invitation
    - (d) Command

Directions (Q. Nos. 11-15) Select the most appropriate option to fill in the blanks.

11. B: I go to Highton Secondary School.

    A : ....

    B : No, It is about 5 kilometres away.
    - (a) Why do you get there?
    - (b) Is it near your house?
    - (c) What is it?
    - (d) Was it a boarding school?

12. A. Your dress is so nice.
    B. ....
    (a) I'll buy another one.
    (b) She is so beautiful.
    (c) Thank you, I have made it myself.
    (d) I like them too.

13. A: May I watch TV now?
    B: No you may not.
    A: Why?
    B: ....
    (a) We'll go for a walk tomorrow.
    (b) You were ill.
    (c) I must stay in bed.
    (d) You'll disturb the kids.

14. A: Mary is out now.
    B: ....
    A: Not far away.
    (a) What did she study?
    (b) Where does she come?
    (c) Where has she gone?
    (d) Where are the girls?

15. A: The new film is splendid.
    B: ....
    (a) Not exactly so.
    (b) He is well.
    (c) Of course she is.
    (d) It's cold.

Directions (Q. Nos. 16-20) Choose the best response.

16. Hey, have a chocolate.
    (a) Thank you
    (b) Fine, thank you
    (c) You're welcome
    (d) Sorry

17. Please don't hang up.
    (a) I don't want to talk to you.
    (b) I have to attend another call.
    (c) Talk later.
    (d) None of the above

18. Oops! I've spilt drink on your dress.
    (a) Don't worry. It'll clean off easily.
    (b) That wasn't nice!
    (c) Oh, please don't mention it.
    (d) I'll buy a new dress.

19. I would like to finish my assignment today.
    (a) Won't you be able?
    (b) Will you be able to?
    (c) Would you be able to?
    (d) None of the above

20. Haven't you put on weight recently?
    (a) No, there isn't.   (b) Yes, I did.
    (c) Yes, I have.   (d) Both (a) and (c)

Writing Skills

Directions (Q. Nos. 1-6) Complete the following story by choosing the correct options to fill in the blanks.

Some ...**(1)**.... in Akbar's court were jealous of Birbal. They asked Akbar permission to let them test Birbal's ...**(2)**.... . Akbar told them to go ahead. One courtier stepped up to Birbal and said, "You are indeed very clever. Surely you can tell me how many crows there are in Agra." Birbal thought for a moment and said, "Give me a week and I shall give you the exact ...**(3)**....". From that evening onwards Birbal was to be seen on the terrace staring out across at the crows that flew by or were perched on various places. A ...**(4)**.... passed and darbar was called once again. The courtier stepped up to ...**(5)**.... and asked the same question to him again. Birbal said to him, "Could you tell me how many hairs there are on your head?" "No", said the man. "I am sorry, then", said Birbal, "For that is exactly how many ...**(6)**.... are there in Agra." Akbar and all the courtiers had a hearty laugh at this.

Moral: Intelligence is strength.

1. (a) people   (b) pupil
   (c) citizens   (d) courtiers

2. (a) wisdom   (b) cleverly
   (c) wiseness   (d) clever

3. (a) quantity   (b) number
   (c) crows   (d) numbering

4. (a) day   (b) month
   (c) week   (d) year

5. (a) Akbar   (b) Birbal
   (c) Courtiers   (d) Birbal's wife

6. (a) sparrows   (b) eagles
   (c) parrots   (d) crows

MESSAGE WRITING

Directions (Q. Nos. 7-10) Complete the message after reading the conversation.

Rajesh: Hello! Is it 991234509?

Ramesh: Yes. I'm Ramesh speaking. What can I do for you?

Rajesh: Well, Ramesh! I'm Rajesh, Rohit's friend.

Ramesh: Oh, I see. Well, brother is not here right now. So how can I help you?

Rajesh: Could you please convey to him that he should bring my practical book today in school as I need it in class today?

Ramesh: That's fine. I'll do that.

Message

15th May, 2020

7 a.m.

...**(7)**...

Rajesh ...**(8)**... in your absence. He wants you to bring his ...**(9)**... to school today. He said it is ...**(10)**... as he needs it.

Ramesh

---

7. (a) Ramesh   (b) Rajesh
   (c) Rohit   (d) Raunak

8. (a) called   (b) rang
   (c) messaged   (d) told

9. (a) notebook
   (b) textbook
   (c) practical book
   (d) class book

10. (a) futile   (b) urgent
    (c) important   (d) necessary

Directions (Q. Nos. 11-14) Complete the message after reading the conversation.

Rosy: Hello! Is it 9035022565?

Rehana: Yes, please. Who's it there?

Rosy: I'm Rosy, a friend of Roma. Where is she?

Rehana: Oh! Sorry. Actually she has forgotten her mobile here. She has gone to the market. Can I help you, please?

Rosy: Oh, sure. In fact, I wanted to convey to her that today's music class\shall be suspended because the teacher is not well. Instead it will be held on Sunday. So she should remember it.

Could you please pass this message to her?

Rehana: Oh! Sure. Thank you.

Rosy: Thank you too.

Message

25th June, 2018

1 p.m.

Roma

Your ...**(11)**... Rosy from music class called in your absence. She called to ...**(12)**... that today's music class has been ...**(13)**... because the teacher is not well. Instead, it will be held on ...**(14)**... . So she wants you to remember it.

Rehana

---

11. (a) colleague   (b) manager
    (c) teacher   (d) friend

12. (a) address you   (b) tell you
    (c) inform you   (d) want you

13. (a) suspended   (b) called
    (c) restricted   (d) held

14. (a) Monday   (b) Sunday
    (c) Saturday   (d) Friday

LETTER WRITING

Directions (Q. Nos. 15-19) Complete the letter by choosing the correct options to fill in the blanks.

14/8, Dharma Colony
Ramgarh

15th January, 2021

The Mayor
Ramgarh

Subject: Complaint regarding the problem of water logging in Dharma Colony

Sir/Madam

I am Raj, a ...**(15)**... of Dharma Colony. The residents of the area are facing a lot of problems due to water logging.

Every year in the monsoon season, the area gets filled with water as the ...**(16)**... system gets choked. We have requested the area ...**(17)**... many times, but the situation is still the same. The residents' lives have become ...**(18)**... as many water—borne diseases have spread. All the houses are ...**(19)**... and we are facing a tough time.

Please consider the issue as serious and find a solution at the earliest.

Yours sincerely

Raj

15. (a) resident   (b) citizen
    (c) person   (d) incharge

16. (a) water   (b) sewer
    (c) drainage   (d) pipe

17. (a) incharge   (b) meeting
    (c) chairperson   (d) committee

18. (a) clean   (b) happy
    (c) miserable   (d) satisfied

19. (a) drown   (b) flooded
    (c) fell   (d) sank

Directions (Q. Nos. 20-24) Complete the letter by choosing the correct options to fill in the blanks.

45, Jan Marg
Delhi,
15th January, 2021
Dear Sanjay

Hi! You are ...**(20)**... to my birthday party on 25th August.

The party will be at Archie's Place, Nehru Park from 4:00 to 7:00 PM. As the ...**(21)**... is based on the 'Spiderman' ...**(22)**..., please wear a dress in red/black color combination. It will be fun as I have arranged a Mask game, a 'Spidey' web game and a never-seen-before neon light and music show. I am very ...**(23)**... as I will wear a special Spidey costume designed by my sister. Please come as it will be good to have your ...**(24)**... . Also, bring your brother Saurav.

Waiting for your confirmation!

Yours truly
Gaurav

20. (a) invitation   (b) called
    (c) messaged   (d) invited

21. (a) celebration   (b) treat
    (c) party   (d) none of these

22. (a) game   (b) theme
    (c) costume   (d) subject

23. (a) excited   (b) Sad
    (c) shocked   (d) angry

24. (a) business   (b) joint
    (c) company   (d) group

PRACTICE SET 

Directions (Q. Nos. 1-5) Read the poem carefully and answer the questions based on the poem.

The morns are <u>meeker</u> than they were,
The nuts are getting brown;
The berry's cheek is plumper,
The rose is out of town.
    The maple wears a gayer scarf,
    The field a scarlet gown.
    Lest I should be old-fashioned,
    I'll put a <u>jewellery</u> on.

1. The poem describes the .... season.
(a) autumn   (b) spring
(c) summer   (d) winter

2. Choose the correct sentence in the context of the poem.
(a) In the autumn, many things in nature change.
(b) In the autumn, nuts start getting brown.
(c) In the autumn, people buy new clothes.
(d) None of the above

3. What does the poet infer about 'the rose'?
(a) The poet wishes that there were still roses in town.
(b) There were roses in town before autumn came.
(c) The rose disappeared because the morning became meeker.
(d) The poet has never seen roses before.

4. Find the most suitable word to replace <u>meeker</u> in the poem.
(a) weak (b) nothing (c) soft (d) gentler

5. Find the most suitable word to replace <u>jewellery</u> in the context of the poem.
(a) rock   (b) stone
(c) ornament   (d) glass

6. Choose the collective noun in the following sentence.
The gang of robbers looted the jewellery shop.
(a) jewellery   (b) robbers
(c) shop   (d) gang

7. Choose the odd one out from the following options.
(a) Honesty   (b) Knowledge
(c) Passion   (d) College

8. Identify the adverb in the following sentence.
You are running fast enough.
(a) You   (b) Enough
(c) Fast   (d) Both (b) and (c)

9. Replace the underlined word with a suitable pronoun.
The class teacher punished <u>Sanjeev and I</u> before the class.
(a) them (b) us (c) you (d) ours

10. Fill in the blank in the sentence given below with the most suitable option.
Every student wants an .... solution of a question than a confusing one.

(a) easier   (b) easy
(c) easiest   (d) ease

11. Find the adjective word in the options. given.
    (a) Power   (b) Powerfully
    (c) Powerful   (d) Powerlessness

12. Find the verb in the sentence.
    A girl plays so many roles in her life.
    (a) plays   (b) many   (c) roles   (d) life

13. Choose the helping verb in the given sentence.
    Everyone has to believe in God.
    (a) to   (b) has
    (c) in   (d) everyone

14. Fill in the blank with correct contraction.
    You will complete your homework today, ...
    (a) Willn't you?   (b) Will'nt you?
    (c) Won't you?   (d) Want you?

15. Fill in the blanks in the sentences given below with the most suitable option.
    What a lovely morning ....
    Why are you feeling bored ....
    (a) (.), (?)   (b) (.), (!)
    (c) (!), (!)   (d) (!), (?)

16. Choose the correct spelling.
    (a) Fishure   (b) Fissure
    (c) Fishar   (d) Fissar

17. Complete the following dialogue.
    A : Do you like to play Holi?
    B : Yes, ...
    (a) I just love the festival
    (b) No, I don't like it
    (c) I don't want to play Holi
    (d) None of the above

18. Find the preposition in the sentence given below.
    It is better to wear woollens in winter.
    (a) to   (b) in
    (c) Both (a) and (b)   (d) None of these

19. Choose the conjunction in the given sentence.
    He will help you if you talk to him.
    (a) to   (b) if   (c) will   (d) him

20. Choose the correct word pair.
    (a) Cup and spoon   (b) Back or forward
    (c) Life or death   (d) Bread in pickles

21. Which one of the following sentences uses article correctly?
    (a) Laughter is a best medicine.
    (b) Laughter is an best medicine.
    (c) Laughter is best medicine.
    (d) Laughter is the best medicine.

22. Replace the underlined word with the correct verb tense form.
    They <u>go</u> to Delhi yesterday.
    (a) goes   (b) went   (c) will go   (d) gone

23. Fill the blank with the correct form of verb .
    Hemant .... in every singing competition of his school every year.
    (a) participates   (b) participate
    (c) will participate   (d) All of these

24. Find out the abstract noun from the given sentence.
    A patient should follow his doctor's advice.
    (a) patient   (b) doctor's
    (c) advice   (d) his

25. Which of the options means, 'a written document of his own life'?

(a) Autobiography (b) Biography

(c) Book (d) Novel

26. Replace the underlined word with the most suitable word from the options.
The student is <u>puzzled</u> with the question and is unable to answer it.

(a) terrified (b) confused

(c) pressurised (d) shocked

27. Choose the synonym of the word 'quarrel'.

(a) War (b) Agreement

(c) Anger (d) Dispute

Directions (Q. Nos. 28 and 29) Choose the antonyms of the given words from the options.

28. Lazy

(a) Lethargic (b) Passionate

(c) Active (d) Fast

29. Mature

(a) Inmature (b) Unmature

(c) Irmature (d) Immature

30. Rearrange the given letters to form a meaningful word.
'Cnsocttur'

(a) Construct (b) Tructcons

(c) Conctrust (d) Tonscruct

31. Rearrange the given words to form a meaningful sentence.
was/Sangeeta/a/book/zoo/in/ reading/the/?

(a) Sangeeta was reading a book in the zoo?

(b) Was Sangeeta reading a book in the zoo?

(c) A book was Sangeeta reading in the zoo?

(d) A book was reading Sangeeta in the zoo?

Directions (Q. Nos. 32-35) Complete the message after reading the conversation.

There is a telephonic conversation between Nikit and Neha. As Neha had to leave for taking part in a dance competition so she leaves a message for her friend Sona.

Neha : Can I speak to Sona?

Nikit : She has gone to market with mom.

Neha : I am her friend Neha. Tomorrow I am going to Delhi with my parents for taking part in a dance competition.

Please ask her to accompany me as it will be a fun if she joins me.

Nikit : I will.

Message

16th June, 2015

......(32)......,

Neha ......(33)...... up to invite you with her for a ......(34)...... competition in Delhi, as she is going with her parents. If you are ......(35)...... in joining her, call her immediately.

Nikit

---

32. (a) Neha (b) Sona (c) Nikit (d) Mom

33. (a) called (b) messaged

(c) wrote (d) told

34. (a) music (b) singing

(c) dance (d) vocal

35. (a) ready (b) eager

(c) free (d) interested

PRACTICE SET 02 

Directions (Q. Nos. 1-5) Read the following passage carefully and answer the questions that follow.

Money is what you use to buy things. You may earn money from completing household chores, getting good grades, for your <u>allowance</u> or for losing a tooth! Money is very important in our world and comes in many different forms.

People have been using money for hundreds of years. Before money gave specific values for things, people simply traded items. In the United States, we use the dollar as our currency or money, but people in different parts of the world use different currencies, though some countries also use or <u>accept</u> our dollars.

People earn money from the jobs they have and use that money to save for the future, pay for their houses, cars, food, taxes, medical needs and household items, among other things. Even things such as keeping the lights on, using the air conditioning or heat and connecting to the internet costs money.

1. According to the passage, people started using money ....
   (a) in the form of dollars
   (b) hundreds of years ago
   (c) thousands of years ago
   (d) as their allowance

2. Money could be used ....
   (a) to pay you for doing your chores
   (b) to save for the future
   (c) Both (a) and (b) are correct
   (d) Both (a) and (b) are incorrect

3. When there was no money people ....
   (a) made everything themselves
   (b) traded to get what they needed
   (c) just never got what they needed
   (d) None of the above

4. Replace <u>allowance</u> with the most suitable word in the context of the passage.
   (a) leave   (b) authority
   (c) payment   (d) approval

5. Find out the antonym of <u>accept</u> in the context of the passage.
   (a) reject   (b) obey   (c) ignore (d) disown

6. Fill in the blank with the most suitable option.
   Now every child has the right to free .... till class 10th.
   (a) food   (b) education
   (c) clothes   (d) transportation

7. Match the following nouns in List-I with their collective nouns in List-II.

List I	List II
A. Elephants	1. Flock
B. Judges	2. Herd
C. Bird	3. Bunch
D. Idiots	4. Panel

Codes

	A	B	C	D		A	B	C	D
(a)	1	2	3	4	(b)	2	4	1	3
(c)	4	3	2	1	(d)	3	1	4	2

8. Fill in the blank with correct pronoun.
Don't push .... so hard, I could be hurt.
(a) him (b) you (c) her (d) me

9. Identify the type of pronoun underlined in the given sentence.
Where do you reside in Delhi? I wish to see you at your residence.
(a) Indefinite, possessive
(b) Interrogative, reflexive
(c) Interrogative, personal
(d) Relative, demonstrative

10. Fill in the blank with an adverb.
He is swimming so ....
(a) effortlessly (b) effortly
(c) deliciously (d) calmly

11. Identify the adjective in the following sentence.
Dhoni is one of the finest players in the world.
(a) one (b) finest
(c) world (d) players

Directions (Q. Nos. 12 and 13) Choose the correct option to fill in the blanks to form meaningful sentences.

12. The Moon .... around the Earth.
(a) rotate (b) will rotate
(c) rotates (d) rotating

13. Why are you being so worried ....
Just read newspaper daily for updates..........
(a) (!), (.) (b) (,), (?)
(c) (?), (.) (d) (?), (!)

14. Choose the helping verb in the following sentence.
Rohan does not bring vegetables from the market.
(a) does (b) not
(c) from (d) bring

15. Choose the word with incorrect spelling.
(a) Brewery
(b) Central
(c) Monster
(d) Creachare

16. Complete the following dialogue.
A : Which monument you want to visit in Delhi?
B : ....
(a) I wanted to visited the Red Fort.
(b) I want to visit the Red Fort.
(c) I did not want to visit the Red Fort.
(d) I will visit the Taj Mahal.

17. Find out the correct preposition from the options given to fill in the blank.
Rahul works in a bank .... an accountant.
(a) so (b) as
(c) or (d) into

Directions (Q. Nos. 18 and 19) Choose the correct conjunction to fill in the blanks.

18. Neither Sita .... Geeta has broken the glass.
(a) or
(b) nor
(c) not
(d) and

19. He is the teacher .... teaches us English.
  (a) who   (b) that
  (c) which   (d) but

20. Choose the correct meaning of the idiom given below.
  A bolt from the blue
  (a) Being sad
  (b) A complete surprise
  (c) Happy moment
  (d) Being angry

21. Choose correct articles to form meaningful sentences.
  There is .... University in Delhi, which is very famous.
  (a) a   (b) the
  (c) no article   (d) All of these

22. Complete the following word analogy.
  Clay : Potter :: Stone : ?
  (a) Editor   (b) Maker
  (c) Sculptor   (d) Inventor

23. Choose the noun in the given sentence.
  There is a huge crowd in the buses on a working day.
  (a) buses
  (b) crowd
  (c) day
  (d) All of these

24. Choose the odd one out from the following options.
  (a) Pond   (b) Aquarium
  (c) River   (d) Lake

Directions (Q. Nos. 25 and 26) Choose the synonyms of the words given below.

25. Enquired
  (a) Asked
  (b) Interrogated
  (c) Answered
  (d) Replied

26. Enemy
  (a) Friend   (b) Foe
  (c) Mate   (d) Supporter

Directions (Q. Nos. 27 and 28) Choose the antonyms of the given words.

27. Insufficient
  (a) Scare   (b) Volume
  (c) Amount   (d) Enough

28. Neat
  (a) Dirty
  (b) Clean
  (c) Disturbed
  (d) Organised

29. Rearrange these letters to form a suitable word.
  tewra
  (a) Tewar   (b) Rewat
  (c) Water   (d) Etraw

30. Rearrange these words to form a suitable sentence.
  we/go/market/bus/used /by/to/to/.
  (a) Bus used to go to market by we.
  (b) Market by bus we used to go to.
  (c) We used to go to market by bus.
  (d) We used to go to bus by market.

Directions (Q. Nos. 31-35) Complete the story by filling the blanks with the most suitable option given below.

Once a lark made her ......**(31)**...... in a corn-field. Soon she laid eggs in it. After a few days small babies hatched out of them.

One day the baby-larks overheard the farmer say,

"I will call my neighbours to reap this field".

The baby-larks got alarmed on hearing this and told their ......**(32)**...... about it.

"Don't worry," said the mother.

Some days later, the farmer came again and said, I will call my relatives to reap this ......**(33)**...... ."

The baby-larks got afraid again.

"Don't ......**(34)**......," said their mother.

But the next day the farmer came there with his little son and said, "I will reap this field tomorrow."

"Now is the time to go. When a man says he will do the work ......**(35)**......, he will certainly do it," said the mother-lark.

31. (a) home   (b) nest
     (c) cage   (d) hut

32. (a) mother   (b) friend
     (c) father   (d) relatives

33. (a) ground   (b) nest
     (c) field   (d) hill

34. (a) fear   (b) afraid
     (c) panic   (d) worry

35. (a) yourself   (b) ourselves
     (c) self   (d) himself

ANSWERS

Chapter 1   Noun

1. (b)	**2.** (a)	**3.** (c)	**4.** (b)	**5.** (c)	**6.** (b)	**7.** (a)	**8.** (a)	**9.** (c)	**10.** (d)
11. (d)	**12.** (b)	**13.** (c)	**14.** (b)	**15.** (d)	**16.** (a)	**17.** (a)	**18.** (a)	**19.** (c)	**20.** (b)
21. (c)	**22.** (c)	**23.** (d)	**24.** (a)	**25.** (b)	**26.** (b)	**27.** (c)	**28.** (a)	**29.** (b)	**30.** (d)
31. (c)	**32.** (d)								

Chapter 2   Pronoun

1. (c)	**2.** (c)	**3.** (c)	**4.** (b)	**5.** (c)	**6.** (d)	**7.** (a)	**8.** (b)	**9.** (b)	**10.** (a)
11. (d)	**12.** (c)	**13.** (a)	**14.** (b)	**15.** (d)	**16.** (c)	**17.** (a)	**18.** (b)	**19.** (b)	**20.** (d)
21. (a)	**22.** (c)	**23.** (d)	**24.** (d)	**25.** (c)	**26.** (b)	**27.** (b)	**28.** (c)	**29.** (b)	**30.** (d)
31. (c)	**32.** (c)	**33.** (b)	**34.** (c)	**35.** (b)	**36.** (d)	**37.** (c)	**38.** (b)	**39.** (d)	**40.** (c)

Chapter 3   Verb

1. (d)	**2.** (a)	**3.** (c)	**4.** (b)	**5.** (a)	**6.** (c)	**7.** (b)	**8.** (a)	**9.** (d)	**10.** (a)
11. (c)	**12.** (d)	**13.** (a)	**14.** (d)	**15.** (c)	**16.** (c)	**17.** (b)	**18.** (d)	**19.** (d)	**20.** (b)
21. (c)	**22.** (b)	**23.** (d)	**24.** (b)	**25.** (c)	**26.** (a)	**27.** (a)			

Chapter 4   Adverbs

1. (c)	**2.** (d)	**3.** (a)	**4.** (b)	**5.** (a)	**6.** (c)	**7.** (d)	**8.** (d)	**9.** (b)	**10.** (a)
11. (c)	**12.** (a)	**13.** (a)	**14.** (c)	**15.** (b)	**16.** (c)	**17.** (a)	**18.** (b)	**19.** (b)	**20.** (d)
21. (a)	**22.** (b)	**23.** (d)	**24.** (c)	**25.** (d)	**26.** (c)	**27.** (d)	**28.** (b)	**29.** (a)	**30.** (c)

Chapter 5   Adjective

1. (c)	**2.** (d)	**3.** (c)	**4.** (c)	**5.** (b)	**6.** (a)	**7.** (b)	**8.** (c)	**9.** (d)	**10.** (d)
11. (b)	**12.** (d)	**13.** (a)	**14.** (c)	**15.** (a)	**16.** (c)	**17.** (a)	**18.** (b)	**19.** (b)	**20.** (c)
21. (a)									

Chapter 6   Articles

1. (d)	**2.** (c)	**3.** (a)	**4.** (a)	**5.** (b)	**6.** (c)	**7.** (c)	**8.** (c)	**9.** (a)	**10.** (d)
11. (c)	**12.** (b)	**13.** (d)	**14.** (d)	**15.** (b)	**16.** (d)	**17.** (b)	**18.** (a)	**19.** (a)	**20.** (b)
21. (a)	**22.** (a)	**23.** (c)	**24.** (a)	**25.** (a)	**26.** (c)	**27.** (c)	**28.** (c)	**29.** (c)	**30.** (c)

Chapter 7   Preposition

1. (a)	2. (b)	3. (c)	4. (d)	5. (b)	6. (b)	7. (c)	8. (a)	9. (c)	10. (b)
11. (b)	12. (c)	13. (c)	14. (b)	15. (c)	16. (b)	17. (d)	18. (a)	19. (b)	20. (d)
21. (a)	22. (d)	23. (c)	24. (b)	25. (c)	26. (a)	27. (c)	28. (d)	29. (b)	30. (c)

Chapter 8   Conjunction

1. (a)	2. (d)	3. (b)	4. (c)	5. (b)	6. (b)	7. (c)	8. (a)	9. (c)	10. (a)
11. (a)	12. (c)	13. (d)	14. (b)	15. (c)	16. (d)	17. (a)	18. (c)	19. (c)	20. (d)
21. (c)	22. (d)	23. (b)	24. (b)	25. (a)	26. (b)	27. (b)	28. (b)	29. (a)	30. (a)
31. (d)	32. (a)								

Chapter 9   Tenses

1. (c)	2. (d)	3. (d)	4. (b)	5. (d)	6. (d)	7. (c)	8. (a)	9. (c)	10. (a)
11. (b)	12. (c)	13. (d)	14. (c)	15. (a)	16. (a)	17. (b)	18. (b)	19. (a)	20. (b)
21. (b)	22. (a)	23. (c)	24. (a)	25. (b)					

Chapter 10   Contractions

1. (a)	2. (d)	3. (d)	4. (c)	5. (c)	6. (b)	7. (a)	8. (b)	9. (a)	10. (b)
11. (a)	12. (d)	13. (c)	14. (b)	15. (c)	16. (b)	17. (d)	18. (a)	19. (b)	20. (b)
21. (d)	22. (c)	23. (a)	24. (b)	25. (c)					

Chapter 11   Punctuations

1. (c)	2. (d)	3. (b)	4. (a)	5. (a)	6. (b)	7. (c)	8. (c)	9. (d)	10. (b)
11. (c)	12. (d)	13. (c)	14. (d)	15. (b)	16. (b)	17. (d)	18. (c)	19. (b)	20. (a)
21. (d)	22. (b)	23. (c)	24. (b)	25. (c)					

Chapter 12   Jumbled Words and Jumbled Sentences

1. (b)	2. (c)	3. (a)	4. (d)	5. (b)	6. (a)	7. (c)	8. (a)	9. (c)	10. (d)
11. (c)	12. (b)	13. (d)	14. (b)	15. (a)	16. (a)	17. (c)	18. (b)	19. (b)	20. (d)
21. (b)	22. (a)	23. (d)	24. (c)						

Chapter 13   Synonyms

1. (b)	2. (b)	3. (c)	4. (d)	5. (a)	6. (a)	7. (b)	8. (c)	9. (d)	10. (d)
11. (b)	12. (c)	13. (c)	14. (c)	15. (d)	16. (c)	17. (b)	18. (a)	19. (a)	20. (d)

Chapter 14   Antonyms

1. (c)	2. (c)	3. (d)	4. (a)	5. (a)	6. (c)	7. (a)	8. (d)	9. (b)	10. (c)
11. (b)	12. (a)	13. (d)	14. (a)	15. (b)	16. (d)	17. (c)	18. (c)	19. (c)	20. (b)
21. (b)	22. (b)	23. (d)							

Chapter 15   One Word Substitution

1. (d)	2. (a)	3. (c)	4. (b)	5. (a)	6. (b)	7. (c)	8. (b)	9. (d)	10. (a)
11. (a)	12. (d)	13. (b)	14. (a)	15. (a)	16. (c)	17. (c)	18. (a)	19. (a)	20. (a)
21. (a)	22. (b)	23. (d)	24. (b)	25. (a)					

Chapter 16   Word Pair and Odd One Out

1. (c)	2. (c)	3. (d)	4. (b)	5. (a)	6. (d)	7. (a)	8. (b)	9. (b)	10. (d)
11. (d)	12. (b)	13. (a)	14. (c)	15. (b)	16. (d)	17. (b)	18. (a)	19. (c)	20. (b)
21. (c)	22. (c)	23. (d)	24. (b)	25. (a)					

Chapter 17   Spellings

1. (b)	2. (d)	3. (a)	4. (c)	5. (a)	6. (b)	7. (a)	8. (c)	9. (b)	10. (d)
11. (a)	12. (c)	13. (b)	14. (a)	15. (c)	16. (b)	17. (a)	18. (b)	19. (c)	20. (b)
21. (a)	22. (c)	23. (b)	24. (d)	25. (b)	26. (c)	27. (d)	28. (b)	29. (a)	30. (c)
31. (c)	32. (a)	33. (b)	34. (a)	35. (c)					

Chapter 18   Idiom, Phrases and Proverb

1. (c)	2. (a)	3. (b)	4. (c)	5. (d)	6. (c)	7. (b)	8. (d)	9. (d)	10. (c)
11. (a)	12. (b)	13. (c)	14. (b)	15. (a)	16. (c)	17. (d)	18. (c)	19. (b)	20. (a)
21. (d)	22. (b)	23. (c)	24. (a)	25. (b)					

Chapter 19   Reading Comprehension

Passage 1	1. (c)	2. (d)	3. (d)	4. (b)	5. (d)	Poem 1	11. (a)	12. (b)	13. (d)	14. (a)	15. (c)
Passage 2	6. (a)	7. (d)	8. (b)	9. (d)	10. (a)	Poem 2	16. (a)	17. (c)	18. (a)	19. (b)	20. (a)

Chapter 20   Spoken and Written Expression

1. (c)	2. (a)	3. (a)	4. (b)	5. (b)	6. (d)	7. (b)	8. (d)	9. (a)	10. (b)
11. (b)	12. (c)	13. (d)	14. (c)	15. (a)	16. (a)	17. (b)	18. (a)	19. (c)	20. (c)

1. (d)	**2.** (a)	**3.** (b)	**4.** (c)	**5.** (b)	**6.** (d)	**7.** (c)	**8.** (a)	**9.** (c)	**10.** (b)
11. (d)	**12.** (c)	**13.** (a)	**14.** (b)	**15.** (a)	**16.** (c)	**17.** (d)	**18.** (c)	**19.** (b)	**20.** (d)
21. (c)	**22.** (b)	**23.** (a)	**24.** (c)						

Practice Set 1

1. (a)	**2.** (a)	**3.** (b)	**4.** (a)	**5.** (c)	**6.** (d)	**7.** (d)	**8.** (d)	**9.** (b)	**10.** (b)
11. (c)	**12.** (a)	**13.** (b)	**14.** (c)	**15.** (d)	**16.** (b)	**17.** (a)	**18.** (c)	**19.** (b)	**20.** (c)
21. (d)	**22.** (b)	**23.** (a)	**24.** (c)	**25.** (a)	**26.** (b)	**27.** (d)	**28.** (c)	**29.** (d)	**30.** (a)
31. (b)	**32.** (b)	**33.** (a)	**34.** (c)	**35.** (d)					

Practice Set 2

1. (b)	**2.** (c)	**3.** (b)	**4.** (c)	**5.** (a)	**6.** (b)	**7.** (b)	**8.** (d)	**9.** (c)	**10.** (a)
11. (b)	**12.** (c)	**13.** (c)	**14.** (a)	**15.** (d)	**16.** (b)	**17.** (b)	**18.** (b)	**19.** (a)	**20.** (b)
21. (b)	**22.** (c)	**23.** (d)	**24.** (b)	**25.** (a)	**26.** (b)	**27.** (d)	**28.** (a)	**29.** (c)	**30.** (c)
31. (b)	**32.** (a)	**33.** (c)	**34.** (d)	**35.** (d)					